The Art of The Argument

The Art of The Argument

Western Civilization's Last Stand

Stefan Molyneux

ISBN: 1548742074
ISBN 13: 9781548742072

CONTENTS

TRIGGER WARNING

This book will help you understand arguments, why they matter - and how to win them. I want you to use the contents of this book to fight for truth and virtue in the real world. "The Art of the Argument" is an outright battle manual, not a prissy abstract academic paper.

Academic logicians have had thousands of years to popularize their terms - validity, soundness, sequents and so on - and have failed completely. Countless texts on formal logic have been penned; to what end? The world is still massively irrational, and most people know nothing of these ivory tower technical terms. As we approach Western Civilization's last stand for survival, loftily lecturing people on arcane terms is a mere confession of pitiful impotence. I cannot for the life of me imagine how our desperate fight for freedom can be won by whining that an enemy's sophistry is "valid but not sound."

State-funded academics have taken your tax money by the billions, while turning logic into wingdings and leaving you utterly undefended.

My goal in this book is to give you the skills and strength to fight a lion, not get you to memorize its Latin name while being eaten alive. I speak as Socrates taught, in the language of the people. Academics may quibble; it is with a sigh and a swig and a swing that we must save them, too.

Triggered yet? I certainly hope so.

Let us begin.

PART ONE: AN INTRODUCTION TO THE ARGUMENT

The first thing to understand is that **The Argument** is *everything*. **The Argument** is civilization; **The Argument** is peace; **The Argument** is love; **The Argument** is truth and beauty; **The Argument** is, in fact, *life itself*.

What do you think of when you hear the word "argument"? Probably nagging spouses, battling coworkers, internet flame-wars, scolding politicians – the kind of win/lose verbal wars that only end when one person cowers in exhaustion and gives up his position.

That is *not* **The Argument**.

The Argument is the rational map that allows us to navigate and meet in reality. **The Argument** keeps us sane by reminding us of facts and reason and evidence. **The Argument** stops wars, abuse, bullying, manipulation and aggression of every kind. **The Argument** is the robust sport that stops hysterical escalation. **The Argument** prevents the scourge of violence: it is the only thing that can.

The Argument favors the intelligent, the prepared, the resourceful, the courageous, and the well-trained. **The Argument** rewards intellectual and moral virtues of every kind. **The Argument** promotes the most civil to the highest reaches of influence in society, and demotes fools and bullies to the basements of irrelevance.

In short, we can embrace **The Argument** and have civilization – or we can reject **The Argument** and descend into a living hell without end.

There is no other choice.

WHAT IS AN ARGUMENT?

An argument is an attempt to convince another person of the truth or value of your position using only reason and evidence. There are two fundamental kinds of arguments – one establishes *truth*, the other establishes *value*.

Truth arguments aim to unite fragmented and subjective humanity under the challenging banner of actual reality. *Truth arguments* wage war against delusion, confirmation bias and the endless emotional reactions currently programmed in the human mind against any facts that challenge profitable prejudice. These are called "hate facts" by those who hate facts.

Value arguments aim at improvements in aesthetic or moral standards – anything from "We should really buy this picture, not that picture," to "Let's go to this movie, rather than that movie," to "The human mind is elevated by exposure to beauty, not ugliness," to "It is preferable to pursue virtue rather than vice," and so on.

A *truth argument* can tell us who killed someone. A value argument tells us that murder is wrong. *Truth arguments* are the court; *value arguments* are the law.

A *truth argument* cares nothing for consequences. A *value argument* cannot be defined by consequences, but cannot be indifferent either. A *truth argument* can establish whether arsenic is present in a drink. A *value argument* can convince you not to serve it to someone.

These two kinds of arguments are not completely independent: for a truth argument to have value, we must value the truth; for a value argument to have meaning, it must be true.

Truth Arguments

Truth arguments are divided into two categories that were once taught to even moderately intelligent people, but which are now mostly withheld from everyone. Children are rarely taught critical thinking anymore, and society has become so antirational that basic reason and evidence are the new counterculture: thought is the new punk.

The first category is called "deductive reasoning," the second is called "inductive reasoning."

The general difference is between *certainty* and *probability*. One way to differentiate them is that, as babies, we learn certainties before we learn probabilities, and "d" comes before "i" in the alphabet.

Deductive Reasoning

Deductive reasoning gives 100% proof, assuming all the premises are correct. Inescapable, perfect, divine proof. The standard example is this:

1. All men are mortal.
2. Socrates is a man.
3. Therefore Socrates is mortal.

Given that premises one and two are true, the conclusion - three - is inescapable. (What this means is that anyone who tries to escape the conclusion is actually trying to escape rationality and reality.)

Naturally, relativists of every stripe and hue will fight against the inescapability of the *conclusion* tooth-and-nail. Getting most modern thinkers to accept the *absolutism of deductive reasoning* is like trying to use a nail-gun to attach electrified Jell-O to a fog bank. Most of us are trained to look for every possible exception to every potential rule – it is a way of evading the responsibility of following basic rules.

However, if you surrender to the peace of absolutism – *if the premises are correct, and the reasoning is correct, the conclusion is absolute and inescapable* – you will quickly find it a beautiful place to be, and that relativists are trying to deny you the peace, Zen, and beauty of the paradise called *certainty*. Take a deep breath, understand this, and your life becomes much simpler and much more effective. Relativism is the air horn that shatters the peace and concentration of reason.

If deductive reasoning leads to a conclusion you disagree with, you are certainly free to deny that conclusion, but your sanity is far better served by examining the premises, rather than blindly rejecting the conclusion.

This is not to say that the sensibility of a conclusion is irrelevant – Aristotle once said that if your moral system somehow proves that murder is a wonderful thing, you've made a mistake somewhere. A negative reaction to a conclusion is like a suspicious coroner's report – it doesn't prove a crime, but it should certainly spur further investigation.

Deductive reasoning is the process of extracting general rules from specific observations, and then applying them to new empirical information. If I notice that some animals are warm-blooded, I can create a category called "warm-blooded," and then sort new animals I find according to this information.

There is a problem of overlapping categories, though, which really needs to be understood. While it is true that all men eat food, not every person who eats food is a man. All ice is cold, but not all cold things are made of ice. Staying alert to this "reverse extrapolation" is very important in

any debate. Drilling down from the general to the specific is enormously helpful – drilling up from the specific to the general is far more challenging – and is in fact the realm of inductive reasoning, which we will get
to shortly.

Examples of Bad Deductive Reasoning

Consider the following:

1. All plumbers can swim.
2. Bob knows how to swim.
3. Therefore Bob is a plumber.

Hopefully, the above argument produces a spark of intellectual short-cir-
cuiting in your brain, since it goes wrong in so many ways.

Of course, not all plumbers can swim, so why bother reading further?

Of course, not everyone who knows how to swim is a plumber - the only
thing that could be provisionally true is the proposition that Bob knows
how to swim.

Does this seem crazy? Here are some more challenges:

1. Kind people are socialists.
2. Bob is a kind person.
3. Therefore Bob is a socialist.

Or:

1. Kind people support the welfare state.
2. Bob is a kind person.
3. Therefore Bob supports the welfare state.

Or, conversely:

1. People are either mean or kind.
2. Only kind people support the welfare state.
3. Therefore only mean people oppose the welfare state.
4. Bob opposes the welfare state.
5. Therefore Bob is a mean person.

Or:

1. People are either mean or kind.
2. Kind people want children to be educated.
3. Only the government can educate children.
4. Bob opposes government education.
5. Therefore Bob opposes children being educated.
6. Therefore Bob is a mean person.

Or:

1. Only mean people want poor people to starve.
2. Only the welfare state prevents poor people from starving.
3. Bob opposes the welfare state.
4. Therefore Bob wants poor people to starve.
5. Therefore Bob is a mean person.

Or:

1. Only mean people want poor people to stay sick.
2. Only government-run healthcare prevents poor people from staying sick.
3. Bob opposes government-run healthcare.
4. Therefore Bob wants poor people to stay sick.
5. Therefore Bob is a mean person.

Does any of this sound familiar? If it doesn't, you probably haven't spent much time arguing for freedom in the public sphere.

It is easy to see how ridiculous these arguments are when broken down into syllogisms, but it is amazing how endlessly these fallacies are replicated in political conversation.

1. People are either mean or nice.
2. Nice people support the government program called "immigration."
3. Bob opposes the government program called "immigration."
4. Therefore Bob is a mean person.

What very few people seem to notice these days is that *there is no actual moral or factual argument in any of the above examples*. Even if Bob *is* a mean person, this has no bearing on the analysis of his position. Can we merely dismiss the arguments of people who might be mean out of hand?

To do so is to destroy the debate by attacking the person rather than **The Argument** – to avoid engaging at any serious intellectual level – which is one of the oldest rhetorical tricks in the book. In fact, it is a rhetorical trick that existed before there *were* books.

(This is in general a tactic of the left, who have become so addicted to this type of verbal abuse that it's hard to imagine how their descending spiral of hateful language might be broken. They revile adversaries in horrible terms, refusing to engage in real debate, all the while shielding their own heroes from legitimate moral criticism.)

Synonym Logic
One form of fairly useless argumentation can be called "synonym logic."

"Synonym logic" occurs when two terms are introduced that seem different but turn out to be the same – you may also refer to this as a "tautology." In my university debating days, the example given was "Coke is it" – where the word "it" turned out to be defined as "coke." This less-than-stellar intellectual achievement of proving that "Coke is coke" is a stirring reminder of Aristotle's first law of logic, but nevertheless remains unimpressive to anyone over the age of four.

This happens more often than you might think. In many religious debates, the word "God" often ends up being defined as "the universe," or "existence." In this context, proving that "god exists" merely ends up proving that "existence exists." Alternatively, "god" can be redefined as "a belief in god," with similar results.

In the realm of political debate, the word "education" generally turns out to mean, "coercively funded government schools," which is not the same thing at all, since education takes many forms. However, by creating this false equivalency, opponents of coercively funded government schools can be easily painted as opposing education as a whole. Equating the words "kindness" and "charity" with "coercively funded government welfare programs" allows for the same sleazy manoeuvre. As Frédéric Bastiat wrote in 1850:

"Socialism, like the ancient ideas from which it springs, confuses the distinction between government and society. As a result of this, every time we object to a thing being done by government, the socialists conclude that we object to its being done at all. We disapprove of state education. Then the socialists say that we are opposed to any education. We object to a state religion. Then the socialists say that we want no religion at all. We object to a state-enforced equality. Then they say that we are against equality. And so on, and so on. It is as if the socialists were to accuse us of not wanting persons to eat because we do not want the state to raise grain."

In the same way, "foreign aid" generally gets defined as "the only possible way to help poor and innocent people in other countries avoid dying from hunger," which pulls the neat linguistic trick of allowing you to accuse anyone sceptical of the value and virtue of foreign aid to be in favour of the innocent starving to death.

Have a look at the following argument:

1. Bob is a bachelor.
2. All bachelors are unmarried men.
3. Therefore Bob is an unmarried man.

While this is valid and sound, what has it really added to the sum total of human knowledge? It amounts to little more than looking something up in a dictionary and saying that the word matches its definition. The phrase "unmarried man" is merely the definition of the word "bachelor," and synonyms do not add much to human knowledge. (Except perhaps for people learning the basics of a new language – precisely those who are not prepared to debate in the first place!)

One of the reasons why clear definitions at the beginning of a debate are so important is that they help you avoid wasting time on "synonym logic."

Limits of Deductive Reasoning

Deductive reasoning works better with concepts than instances. The biological category "dogs" is partially defined as mammals with four legs, but of course not all individual dogs have four legs, due to accidents, mutations, disease and so on. Also, equally obviously, not everything with four legs is a mammal – lizards, tables etc.

Overlapping categories are even more confusing to many people. Every time I make the case that atheists tend to be leftists, a kind of *spergy* category confusion erupts into random geysers of emotional defensive-ness: *"Not all atheists are leftists!"* *"Atheism is not a political category!"* *"I am an atheist and I am not on the left, so your argument is invalid!"*

These kinds of trends can be very confusing to people who don't under-stand basic reasoning. Consider the following case:

1. Atheists tend to be leftists.
2. In a democracy, people tend to vote according to their political beliefs.
3. Therefore, in a democracy, as atheism tends to increase, leftist policies tend to increase.

When laid out in this fashion, things are not so terribly complicated, are they? The confusion tends to stem from an emotional overreaction and a simple lack of reading comprehension. When an argument is made for a tendency, replying with the counterexample is not an argument, but a confession of fundamental – usually overemotional – intellectual illiteracy. If I say Danish people tend to be tall, replying that you know a short Danish person merely serves as your confession that you do not know what the term "tend" means.

CORRELATION AND CAUSATION

Of course, the fact that atheists tend to be leftists does not necessarily mean that atheism *causes* leftism in politics. The causality could go the other way, in that leftism in politics causes atheism; or, there could be some other causality that affects both. Perhaps a belief in Darwinian evolution triggers both leftism and atheism. (*Since the poor are denied rewards in heaven, we must give them money here on earth.*)

It is certainly possible to come up with theories to try to explain this kind of causality. For instance, Christianity generally opposes massive government growth, since for Christians, free will is essential for morality, and government coercion strips citizens of free will. Thus, if you want to increase the size and power of the state, Christianity generally stands in your way.

Atheists also tend to prefer consequentialism, or outcome-based moral standards. That which produces direct and immediate benefits in society is considered the good: the greatest good for the greatest number, and so on. These are not principled arguments, but pragmatic arguments. The *principled* argument against the welfare state is that it violates property rights (thou shalt not steal). The *consequentialist* argument for the welfare state is that it immediately reduces the amount of poverty in society. If your goal is consequentialist, principled arguments often stand in your way. Religious morality tends to operate on abstract principles rather than material consequences, which is why there are the *10 Commandments*, rather than the *10 Government Policy Proposals That Rapidly Alleviate Particular Suffering Among Targeted Groups in Society.*

Atheism may be promoted by those wanting to increase state power, since it removes the obstacle of Christianity - one example of this would be communism. If one goal of atheism as an ideology is to expand state power, then we would expect atheists – who generally claim to be scientific – to reject scientific or moral claims that reduce state power. When talking to atheists about global warming scepticism, racial differences in intelligence or cutting government funding for science, I have found that most are quite hostile to such arguments.

People often reject a claim of association by chanting the mantra that *correlation does not equal causation.* However, if you review the syllogisms above regarding atheist leftism, you will note that no causation is stated. If you do not make an argument for causation, your argument cannot be rejected for failing to prove causation.

However, it often will be.

The Difference Between 'Logical' and 'True'

An argument may be logical – the conclusion follows from the premises – but still be false if the premises are wrong. If I say...

1. All men are immortal
2. Socrates is a man
3. Therefore Socrates is immortal

then the structure remains logically valid. The conclusion *does* follow from the premises, in that all instances represented by a category must share the characteristics of that category – in this case, the immortality of men. But the conclusion is false because *premise one* is false.

Debates often go seriously wrong because the participants tussle about the *conclusion* without examining the premises and **The Argument**. I have for many years repeatedly stated that philosophy is a *process*; the conclusion is largely irrelevant. A factory is a *process* that produces a *product*: a car factory produces a car. An argument is a process that produces a conclusion: the conclusion is not the process, just as a car is not the factory.

The conclusion is irrelevant to the process because the conclusion is a passive product of the process. If you design a factory to produce a car, the factory will produce a car. The factory is the active process; the car is the passive result. In the same way, reason and evidence are the active process; the *conclusion* is the passive result.

The production of cars is the purpose of the car factory – indeed, it is the entire *point* of the car factory. In the same way, the conclusion is the purpose of **The Argument**. If the factory is supposed to produce a car, but instead produces a boat, the process of the factory production needs to be examined and changed. There is little point in criticizing the boat for not being a car, or pretending that the boat is somehow a car. Fix the process; don't merely debate the outcome.

The car factory produces cars for the purpose of profit, which requires the happiness of consumers. **The Argument** produces truth for the purpose of happiness, which requires the integrity of the debaters.

The Argument is like a statue; the conclusions are merely the shadow cast by the statue. There is no point trying to shift the shadow without moving the statue.

The conclusion is the juiciest part of **The Argument** – philosophy's "money shot," so to speak – which is why everyone wants to wrangle about the conclusion. But anyone who jumps in at the deep end in this way, should be disqualified from debating.

Now we move to the second – and generally more common and useful form of reasoning – called "inductive reasoning."

Inductive Reasoning

Inductive reasoning attempts to draw general rules from specific instances. It requires observation first, and cannot be reasoned from first principles. It deals more with *probability* than *certainty*.

These two methodologies are not entirely distinct - think of them as two overlapping circles.

1. There are certainties unrelated to probabilities (gravity).
2. There are probabilities unrelated to certainties (genetics, weather).
3. There are certainties related to probabilities ("I will certainly die if I drown, and I'm more likely to drown if I swim too far.").
4. There are probabilities related to certainties ("I should probably bring an umbrella, even though I am not absolutely certain it will rain.").

To start thinking about inductive reasoning, imagine I'm describing the properties of another world – *Planet Bob* – and I tell you that it often rains when the "*bobbledingles*" are swollen. Would you know this to be true, or false? Even if I tell you that *bobbledingles* are a kind of plant, does that definition help you determine the truth or falsehood of my assertion?

Of course not.

Now, if I tell you that gravity is a property of matter, and *Planet Bob* is composed of matter, would you know for certain that gravity existed in this other world?

Of course you would.

The second statement is an example of deductive reasoning:

1. Gravity is a property of all matter.
2. *Planet Bob* is composed of matter.
3. Therefore *Planet Bob* has the property of gravity.

On the other hand, you can't tell anything about the probability of rain when the plant "*bobbledingles*" is swollen. How would you determine the truth or falsehood of my assertion that it often rains when the "*bobbledingles*" are swollen?

You would have to suit up, fly through space until you got to Planet Bob, find some "*bobbledingles*," and start your observations. There is no other direct way to verify or reject what I have said.

Do you see the difference?

To help us remember why there are two kinds of reasoning, think of the difference between *predator* and *prey*.

A predator must be absolute in its reasoning. The lion must correctly identify and stalk the zebra, must calculate speed and interception without error, must attack and bite accurately, and must persist until the prey is down. All this must serve the conclusion: the meal.

However, *prey* has a different set of calculations because a predator can see the prey, but the prey usually cannot see the predator – at least until it is too late.

A zebra grazing in tall grass must be constantly alert to signs of a predator. However, most signs should be disregarded, for the simple reason that if a zebra sprints off every time the grass moves, it will quickly run out of energy, be more visible because it moves, and be too tired to run if there is a real predator.

Thus the zebra must be alert to its surroundings, accumulating evidence of potential predation, but must not constantly waste energy fleeing without probable cause.

The lion calculates *absolutes*, while the zebra calculates *probabilities*.

This is the difference between deductive and inductive reasoning.

In a very real sense, deductive reasoning is empirical, while inductive reasoning is mathematical. Deductive reasoning is absolute; inductive reasoning analyzes trends.

This is not to say that either one is more important than the other: if the lion is wrong, it does not eat; if the zebra is wrong, it gets eaten.

If you have ever hunted, you know that you possess far more knowledge than your prey. You train your gunsight on a deer as it blissfully eats. If you make a sudden noise, the deer will look up quickly, but then you hold still, hoping to lull it back into a false sense of security.

You are dealing in absolutes – the deer, the gun, the kill – while the deer is dealing with probabilities. What are the odds that the sound is a predator, or just a rabbit, or the wind, or a tree branch creaking? The deer can't run every time it hears a sudden sound, but it must stay alert.

Deductive reasoning goes from the general to the specific – *Socrates is mortal* – because that is what predators do. If you were to program a lion with syllogisms, it might come out something like this:

1. I am hungry.
2. My hunger is satisfied with meat.
3. All zebras are made of meat.
4. The slowest zebras are the easiest to catch.

5. I will stalk and chase the slowest zebra.
6. This zebra is the slowest zebra; I will stalk and chase this one.

You see how this works? The lion is going from the general to the specific – from all zebras to one particular zebra that satisfies the criterion for appeasing the lion's hunger.

In the example above using Socrates and mortality, we go from the mortality of all men to the particular mortality of one individual, just as the lion goes from the potential tastiness of all zebras to the particular taste of the zebra he killed.

Remember, the exchange is not entirely black and white: some probability processing occurs in the mind of the lion, just as some absolutist reasoning occurs in the mind of the zebra. These are general trends that can help you remember the difference between the two ways of approaching data.

Inductive Versus Deductive: Reactionary Versus Proactive

Another admittedly broad generalization regarding the two types of reasoning is the difference between *proactive* and *reactive* behaviors. The lion stalking the zebra is engaged in proactive behavior, and thus, by initiating the encounter, is in far greater control of the variables. You initiate behavior in order to achieve some goal, and you must believe there is a reasonable chance of achieving that goal in order to justify the initial behavior. (You might respond that many people play the lottery, but very few people win. But the point of buying a lottery ticket is the excitement and hope. The man who buys a lottery ticket is almost 100% sure he can achieve his goal: not of winning the lottery, but of buying the ticket.)

Initiating action requires the certainty of deductive reasoning, and control over variables increases that certainty. (The zebra initiates action by eating grass, of course, but there is little chance the grass is going to escape.)

On the other hand, what happens when you try to decide whether to carry an umbrella on a walk? When you look at the sky and check the weather you are being *reactive*. In the same way, the zebra is constantly scanning its surroundings for evidence of imminent predation, like a feminist at a frat party. If a lion leaps at the zebra, the zebra will run, which is *reactive*, not *proactive*. Since deductive reasoning deals more with absolutes, and inductive reasoning deals more with probabilities, inductive reasoning is more focused on how you will *react* to uncertain events.

If you don't want to get wet on your walk, and it is currently raining, you will take an umbrella. You don't need to weigh probabilities, because the event you are trying to decide about is already upon you. A cautious deer has not yet run from the hunter; but after the first gunshot, it flees because the event is already upon it. The pursuit of the lion is the initiating action, the flight of the zebra is the reaction.

This is why I talk about deductive reasoning being predatory, or alpha, while inductive reasoning is prey-based, or beta.

Dominant life forms revel in absolutes and fight hard against any encroaching fumes of rank relativism. A tiger cannot hunt if it doubts the evidence of its senses. The life of a zebra is a life of doubt, of fear.

Absolutism and Society

Parasitical or dependent people often fear and hate absolutes, since they are always weighing costs, benefits, and probabilities: their parasitism can be destroyed by absolutes – particularly moral absolutes.

Think of an abusive woman and her beaten-down husband: she is the predator; he is the prey. She initiates; he reacts. She twists values to damn him and excuse herself. Those who feed him spine-stiffening absolutes are her natural foes, since they help him to stand up to her abuse and free himself from her manipulations.

She feeds him doubt; he is freed by absolutes.

Assertiveness in the animal kingdom generally means killing and eating, which is not the case at all in a civilized human society. The establishment and promulgation of rational absolutes is the very definition of civilization, no matter how scary it may feel to bipedal dependent relativists.

At a rate that has been conservatively clocked at about 10 million instances per minute – at least on the Internet – the following interaction occurs:

1. A generalization is made (inductive reasoning).
2. A specific example is produced rebutting the generalization (deductive response).
3. The generalization is believed to be rebutted.

For instance, when I cite scientific studies detailing a particular tendency among women, the inevitable pushback is that *not all women are like that*. (This is such a common response that it has even coined its own word, the acronym NAWALT.)

Straw-manning a *tendency* as an *absolute* is idiotic.

Inductive Reasoning and Probability

Inductive reasoning moves from general observations to specific probabilities, rather than from general rules to specific instances.

Inductive reasoning takes a gathered set of general observations and attempts to apply a rational theory to explain them. For instance, people tend to carry more umbrellas on cloudy days than on sunny days. Since clouds do not directly compel people to carry umbrellas, it must be a preconceived idea that causes such behavior (in this case, the idea that it cannot rain on a sunny day).

Now, if you tell someone that you notice that more people carry umbrellas on cloudy days, and he replies that *he* never carries an umbrella, he is simply removing himself from the realm of rational argument and revealing himself to be either an idiot, or ridiculously overemotional (two sides of the same coin). Heave a sigh, give him some edible glue, and move on.

Some truths are a complex dance between inductive and deductive reasoning. Deductive reasoning moves from definition to instance, while inductive reasoning moves from instances to generalities.

The root of deductive reasoning is inductive reasoning. As children, we come to understand the definition of "chair" through repeated exposure to chairs. We understand that the sun warms our face because that's what it does, repeatedly. We use inductive reasoning to develop abstract models derived from sensory data, in order to extrapolate immediate experience into general principles.

(There is another category called abductive reasoning that draws a tentative hypothesis from disparate data, but which is related to some sort of testable hypothesis, rather than the reaching of a specific conclusion.)

Examples of Inductive Reasoning

Inductive reasoning draws tentative conclusions from observable patterns: such a conclusion is called a *conjecture*.

Strong conjectures come about when two criteria are met:

1. Significant data is collected.
2. Causality is established.

Let us suppose you get off a plane in Beijing for the first time in your life, and the first thing you see is a man blowing his nose into a garbage can. Would you be justified in texting your friends that everyone in China blows their noses into garbage cans?

No, because you have not collected enough data.

In general, anyone who claims that an absolute can result from inductive reasoning is wrong. You may arrive at absolutes from deductive reasoning, but rarely if ever from inductive reasoning.

Let's say you get a new neighbor, who tells you she has 20 cats. In her backyard, you see 19 black cats with white paws roaming around. If you had to guess, what color would you predict the unseen twentieth cat is?

You have enough data to create a conjecture that the missing cat is also black with white paws, as 95% of her cats – the ones you can see – demonstrate 100% color conformity.

Of course, you cannot prove this for certain, but the conjecture is reasonable. If a million dollars went to the person who correctly guessed the color of the 20th cat, what would you say?

Not only do you have enough data, but you can also create reasonable theories regarding causality.

One possibility is that the causality is entirely random, which is to say that there is no particular causality at all. The fact that the cats have the same color pattern might be pure coincidence, but that is unlikely and easily dismissed.

Here are some causal explanations that spring to mind:

1. Your neighbor has a fetish for black cats with white paws.
2. Whoever provides her cats has a fetish for black cats with white paws.

3. If her cats breed and do not produce black kittens with white paws, she gives them away.
4. The colour pattern is highly transmittable genetically.

If you have causality, and enough data, your conjecture becomes very strong.

Let's say that all the polar bears you see hunting in the snow have white fur. You have some data (all visible polar bears have white fur), and you can create conjectures regarding causality: bears with white fur are harder to see against the snow. This allows them to surprise and kill more prey, making them more likely to survive and reproduce.

When you have clear causality *and* significant data, your conjecture becomes very strong. But it is still enormously difficult to come up with any absolutes through inductive reasoning alone.

Let us say that you have always lived on a beach in Jamaica. You have never seen a polar bear frolicking in the surf. Does this mean it is impossible? Perhaps a passing zoo ship lost a polar bear overboard, or someone's pet polar bear got loose – there are many improbable ways a polar bear might end up frolicking on a beach in Jamaica.

Thus you cannot say that it is *impossible* to find a polar bear frolicking on a beach in Jamaica.

However, you *can* say that polar bears are not native to Jamaica. This returns you to the realm of deductive reasoning, much to the relief of those made anxious by tentative conclusions:

1. Polar bears are native to cold climates.
2. Jamaica is a hot climate.
3. Thus, polar bears are not native to Jamaica.

Or, more specifically:

1. Polar bears are native to cold climates.
2. Jamaica is a hot climate.
3. Thus, *this* polar bear is not native to Jamaica.

Ah, the sweet joy of absolutes, deductive-style!

This is the value that deductive reasoning offers to the gathering of data. If you see a polar bear frolicking on the beach in Jamaica, you know for certain that it is not native to Jamaica. How it got there is another question, but you know it did not evolve there.

This can be very helpful, and even life saving. Knowing that the polar bear is not native to Jamaica might spur you to capture and relocate it to a cooler environment where it can survive.

When you gather enough data and formulate a strong enough theory of causality, you can create a fairly bulletproof conjecture. However, the moment that the conjecture moves from "probable" to "certain" is the moment you generally transition from inductive reasoning to deductive reasoning – from "likely" to "absolute".

To some degree at least, the goal of human knowledge is to move as much information as possible from "theory/conjecture" to "fact." The more we can be certain of, the less we have to think about. The more that we *can* prove, the less we have *to* prove.

In other words, once you learn how to walk, hopefully you will never have to learn how to walk again.

The scientific method is an example of deductive reasoning:

1. All valid hypotheses must be logically consistent
2. All valid hypotheses must conform with – and predict – empirical data.

Individual hypotheses are usually developed according to inductive reasoning – *i.e.* some pattern is observed (an apple falls from a tree) and a logical hypothesis (gravity) is proposed – which is then tested against new empirical data.

The scientific method is absolute – deductive – but individual hypothesis are usually conditional. If new data contradicts the hypothesis, it must be amended.

Inductive reasoning must be subject to the absolutes of deductive reasoning.

INDUCTIVE REASONING AND CERTAINTY

We all thirst for certainty for the simple reason that certainty allows us to move forward. I am certain that I know how to climb stairs, so I can think about other things while doing so. I am certain that two and two make four, so I don't need to endlessly revisit the question.

Having certainties is like the foundation to a house. You can't really build a place to live until the foundation is complete.

There are two ways to achieve certainty: dogma and philosophy. Dogma is by far the easiest choice, of course, and while it may give you the illusion of certainty, it does not give you the reality of knowledge.

Dogma arises, like most dysfunctions, from a greed for the unearned. Dogma results from investing certainty in a *conclusion*, not a *methodology*. In fact, dogmatic people usually end up extremely hostile to the philosophical methodology of reason and evidence.

We must build our certainties on the rocks of philosophy, not the sands of dogma.

If you choose philosophy, you must pass through the valley of the shadow of death called *uncertainty*, or doubt, before arriving at the sunlit plains of certainty. In the field of morality this is called "humility." Uncertainty can be unpleasant, but it is the fiery doorway we must crawl through to arrive at legitimate knowledge.

Many people look at the rigors of rational scepticism and imagine that they lead to a foggy unreality of eternal doubt. David Hume, the famous Scottish philosopher, did not help this cause by introducing the concept of Humean scepticism, or the idea that you cannot get an "ought" from an "is."

While it is true that cutting off a man's head will kill him, there is nothing in the basic biology that tells us we *ought not to do it*: in other words, there is no morality in physics.

While this is true, it is irrelevant to both morality and philosophy.

There is no such thing as *logic* in material physics either, but we do not think that logic is unnecessary or irrelevant or subjective. There is no such thing as "life" in a carbon atom; this does not mean that our own personal accumulation of atoms is not alive.

Gravity existed for billions of years before human thought, and there is nothing in gravity that says that human beings *ought* to develop a theory about gravity. But this does not mean that human ideas about gravity are irrelevant, subjective or unnecessary.

The magic word to introduce here is "if."

If you want to say something true about reality, what you say must be rational, empirical and objective – three sides of the same coin, so to speak.

If you make a claim about reality that is anti-rational, anti-empirical and subjective, your claim is incorrect, since it does not match the properties of empirical reality, which are rational, empirical and objective.

If I accurately want to describe the color red to a child, I must use the word "red."

Nothing in the "redness" of an object commands me to use the word "red," but if I want to be accurate, I must use the word "red."

Also, considering Hume's argument that you cannot get an "ought" from an "is," we can easily see that the mirror of **The Argument** destroys **The Argument**. If we cannot get an "ought" from an "is," then anyone who tries to argue that we *can* is wrong. In other words, we "ought not" get an "ought" from an "is."

Arguing that we cannot derive *universally preferable behavior* from mere matter and energy argues that it is universally preferable behavior to not derive an "ought" from an "is."

If we cannot derive an "ought" from an "is," this means that we can derive an "ought" from an "is," which is that we ought not try it: a self detonating argument.

In the realm of morality – (see my free book on the subject, *Universally Preferable Behaviour: A Rational Proof of Secular Ethics*, available at www. freedomainradio.com/free) – we cannot deny that there is such a thing as universally preferable behavior without already accepting the idea that truth, logic, conformity to reality, and adherence to facts are universally preferable behaviors. I cannot rationally impose upon you my subjective personal preferences, but I can rationally impose upon you the reality that the world is a sphere, or that two and two make four, or that Saturn revolves around the sun.

When we remind people of reality, we are not imposing our will, just presenting facts. Telling you that you are sunburned does not make me the sun.

It is the very universality of philosophy that provides its ethical framework.

Human beings can logically have a universal preference for respecting property rights, for instance, but human beings cannot logically have a universal preference for stealing, for the simple reason that a violation of property rights requires a simultaneous affirmation and denial of property rights. You cannot steal from a man an object he is willing to give you. You can only steal from him if he does not want you to take his property. The act of "theft" only occurs when property rights are affirmed and denied at the same time. If I really want you to steal something from me, then it is not theft, which is why "theft" cannot be universally preferable behavior.

Think of a thief who has just stolen your wallet. The thief desperately wishes to retain ownership of your wallet, at least until he can profit from its contents. If the thief subscribes to a moral theory that argues property rights should be respected, then he damns himself for stealing your wallet. If the thief subscribes to a moral theory that argues property rights should be violated, then he cannot complain if someone steals the wallet from him. But surely he would complain, highlighting the antirational hypocrisy of such contradictory standards. In fact, if the thief knew in advance that the wallet he stole would immediately be stolen from him, he would not bother stealing it in the first place. The thief steals your wallet under the assumption that he can retain control over it. He violates your just property rights even as he strives to maintain his unjust property rights.

If I voluntarily consent to being assaulted by entering a mixed martial arts cage, playing professional hockey, or attending a conservative speech on a California campus, then I cannot be considered the victim of assault. In other words, if I have consented to the assault, it is not assault. (By the way, I am just joking about attending a conservative speech on a California campus – that's assault.)

If I have some sexual fetish role-play fantasy about being raped, and I then ask my partner to simulate such an attack, I cannot reasonably charge my partner with rape. My prior consent means it cannot be considered a crime.

Everyone the world over, and throughout time, can consistently respect personal and property rights, simply by not stealing, murdering, raping or assaulting people, but it is impossible for such violations to be universally preferable, since the universal preference would immediately remove them as an offense.

You might argue that no one should have universal preferences, but you defeat yourself in the statement, since you would be arguing that it is universally preferable behavior for people to have no universally preferable behaviors. In other words, people should follow the universally preferable behavior that there is no such thing as universally preferable behavior.

Since we cannot argue against universally preferable behavior, only one question remains: *which actions constitute logically consistent and empirically verified universally preferable behaviors?*

As mentioned above, thousands of years ago Aristotle remarked that it doesn't really matter what logical gymnastics you go through in establishing your moral system. If the system can be used to justify rape, theft, assault and murder, you've made a mistake somewhere.

As it turns out, *universally preferable behavior* proves that rape, theft, assault and murder are immoral (which is very good, since I agree with Aristotle). It also conforms to empirical evidence showing that as violations of persons and property increase, people suffer and die in escalating numbers (think communism, fascism, socialism etc.), which is significant empirical support for the theory.

Our need for certainty – and this is not just an emotional need, but a practical requirement for living together in a civilized society – has driven us to leap over the challenges of Humean scepticism into the false absolutism of religious edicts and ever-accumulating government laws.

Religious edicts may be fair and just – many are – but they do not conform to the rigorous requirements of philosophical arguments.

Government laws may be fair and just – some are – but they do not conform to the rigorous requirements of philosophical arguments.

Neither mysticism nor governments are part of **The Argument**.

Superstition and state power all diminish as **The Argument** grows and strengthens.

We in the present need certainty. Those in the future need us to earn our certainty *honestly*.

Inductive Reasoning and Philosophy

Individual polar bears may frolic on the beach in Jamaica, but polar bears *as a species* may not. Individual women may be taller than individual men, but women *as a gender* may not be taller than men as a gender.

Since clouds may produce rain, it may rain when it is cloudy, but it will never rain when it is not cloudy.

Inductive reasoning recognizes that patterns are not absolutes unless they can be moved into *categories*. Concepts can be absolutes, instances cannot be. Moving the aggregated information of sense data and experience into absolute concepts – moving from data to conjecture to absolute, or from sense impression to inductive reasoning to deductive reasoning – is the true path of philosophy. (Of course, since all objective human mental disciplines fall under the umbrella of philosophy, this is true for mathematics and science and so on as well.)

Philosophy is the process of moving patterns of experience into universal absolutes, which apply in all places, for all time.

I throw a ball. It arcs up and down, and you catch it, according to the laws of gravity and momentum and friction. I don't need to know any of these laws to catch the ball, any more than a dog needs to understand physics to snatch a frisbee from the air, but nonetheless our direct sense experience can be translated into universal concepts that are absolute across time and space. Gravity works the same on Jupiter as it does on earth.

In society, as it stands, there is great profit in confusion, or a lack of established conjecture, and the avoidance of cause-and-effect in particular. Thinking back to the debate about the dangers of smoking in the 1950s, it was clear that cigarette companies had a multibillion-dollar motivation to oppose the establishment of the correlation between smoking and disease.

In the same way, leftist antipoverty advocates make **The Argument** that poverty breeds crime and other dysfunctions. Thus if we give poor people money, they will become law-abiding citizens, or at least better people.

By promulgating this conjecture, these advocates trigger the transfer of trillions of dollars, which gives them massive incentives to oppose anyone who criticizes or questions this conjecture. See, for example, their reaction to someone who argues that it is not poverty that breeds crime, but rather the presence of crime that breeds poverty. Or someone who argues that lower marriage rates give rise to both poverty and crime. Since the welfare state tends to promote single motherhood, it is the welfare state that increases the prevalence of crime and other dysfunctions in society.

The old phrase "who benefits?" is directly applicable here. When you encounter strong or even violent opposition to your argument, just follow the money. Half the time your opposition is driven by direct financial incentives or an addiction to the power of political compulsion. The rest of the time your opposition is driven by those who desire to normalize dysfunctional personal relationships.

THE ARGUMENT AND CORRECTION

Human beings have a deeply seated desire to correct others. We can be noble and say that this is for the cause of moral instruction and the improvement of the minds and choices of others across the globe – and on occasion this may actually be the case. But the reality is that human beings like to correct other human beings because it is a non-violent way to control them.

The Argument is generally about resource allocation – everything from where your family should go on vacation to how best to help the poor – and if you can convince someone to give you resources, that is a very effective transfer.

For institutions, the general structure of resource transfers goes as follows:

1. Set up a conceptual entity as the highest moral good.
2. Rely on the fact that said conceptual entity cannot speak for itself.
3. Convince people that *you* speak on behalf of that conceptual entity.
4. Claim that that conceptual entity needs resources.
5. Take the money.

In modern, largely secular democracies, this conceptual entity is often described as "the common good" or "the will of the people" and so on. In theocratic societies, it is usually the local ruling deity. In monarchical societies, it is the will of the gods, who chose the king or queen to rule over the masses. In totalitarian societies, it is the class or the race or the nation. It doesn't really matter what brand of conceptual entity is presented, as long as the people believe that it is the highest moral good, and it cannot speak for itself.

In the voluntary realm, the transfer of resources through charity requires the following conditions:

1. Something bad has happened to Person A.
2. Person A was not responsible for the bad thing that happened.
3. Therefore, the bad thing could as easily have happened to Person B.
4. Thus Person B should give resources to Person A, out of empathy.

While bad things *do* happen to people through no fault of their own, the simple economics of the transaction requires that people be paid for having no responsibility. (The fact that we have seen the growth of the welfare state alongside the rise of determinism is no accident.)

The modern cult of victimhood – where every conceivable party (except white males) – seems to have a universal grievance and claims powerlessness – is a mere response to the fact that being a victim in the modern world pays so well, and grants the "powerless" significant political influence and power. Through the state, the illusion of helplessness breeds very real control.

In the political realm, **The Argument** runs this way:

1. Bad things happen to certain groups.
2. Those groups are not responsible for the bad things that happen to them.
3. Only the government can provide charity and restitution.
4. So pay up!

Whatever you subsidize, you increase – whatever you tax, you decrease. Subsidizing helplessness, while taxing productivity, drains society of resources in the long run.

This is an example of how **The Argument** is often little more than a cover for the transfer of resources. Human beings, like all animals, are generally amoral resource acquirers, and one of the most effective methods of safely gaining resources is through **The Argument**, which is why **The Argument** so quickly escalates to hysterical denunciation and defensiveness.

Particularly in politics, once an argument for transferring resources to a particular group is established, those resources become both the figurative and literal lifeblood of many in that group. Single mothers have children largely because the welfare state and other government mechanisms transfer hundreds of billions of dollars to single mothers. (We know this because, as the welfare state has grown, so has the prevalence of single motherhood – and, on the rare times that benefits are curtailed, additional births decline as well.)

Should the welfare state stop, single mothers would find a way to survive, and indeed would most likely flourish. They could find a man to marry and take care of them, or could set up collectives wherein each mother would take care of the other mothers' children on a rotating basis, freeing up their friends to work, and so on. Viewed from the amniotic security of the welfare state, however, such changes may seem apocalyptic: they would be fought tooth-and-nail by all groups that perceive their very lifeblood to be draining from the unclenching fists of state power.

A single mother by definition comes to a relationship with liabilities, which are the costs of her children, and her general unavailability while she is actually raising her children. These liabilities lower her sexual market value enormously. If her value is artificially propped up by the welfare state, her value in the romantic market place is increased, since her liabilities decrease. (In some circumstances, she may actually be an economic net benefit to a boyfriend, particularly if he is unemployed.)

For obvious biological and evolutionary reasons, social decisions that (at least temporarily) reduce people's sexual market value will be opposed vociferously, and sometimes violently. Our genes always struggle to survive and have often developed emotional reactions within us that aid in that survival: anything that threatens the transmission of genes is rightly considered predatory, at least by our DNA.

Thus, **The Argument** is really about controlling *resources* by controlling *human beings*. Universal helplessness cannot be promoted, because helpless people do not create productive resources that can be taken and transferred. If I am a good, decent, hard-working person, and accept a particular set of values, I will almost inevitably follow those values, and fight anything that opposes them. Since I am conscientious, decent and hard-working, I am also generally creating resources through my labor, which makes me well worth controlling.

In a free market, helpless people tend to be poor, while ambitious people tend to be rich. There is a sickly market for selling helpless people the idea that they are poor because the ambitious and wealthy people have stolen resources from them. This creates a dangerous hatred for the productive that sets society on the path to self-destruction.

(There are growing exceptions in the decreasingly free markets of the modern West - wealth is now often achieved through political control of currency, interest rates and access to state control of the economy.)

Energetic actors in a free market tend to produce the most wealth, and successfully producing wealth in the free market requires a challenging combination of assertiveness and empathy. As an entrepreneur, you need to be empathetic to the needs of your customers in order to better serve their needs and win their business. On the other hand, you also need to be assertive – and sometimes downright aggressive – in order to gather the resources you need, fight off competition and lead your team to market victory.

Hard work, dedication and a relentless focus on customer satisfaction can be considered significant virtues, as long as they play out in a voluntary free-market environment. They do not fall exactly into the category of moral virtues, but in terms of practical efficiency, such positive habits carry great power.

On the other hand, in a political environment, hard work, dedication and a relentless focus on customer satisfaction can corrupt people utterly, as they focus on pleasing donors and lying to voters.

Free, conscientious people produce the most resources, and they are often the most susceptible to handing those resources over, which is why moral arguments are so often used to control good people.

In this context, replacing **The Argument** with sophistry is the lifeblood of the dependent, and so often the death of many practical virtues.

FREEDOM AND THE ARGUMENT

The Argument takes many forms beyond formal and structured intellectual debates. Here are some other examples:

- Children negotiating for candy
- Negotiating for a vacation at work
- Discussing where to go on that vacation with your loved ones
- Negotiating the cost of a car, or a house, or any other good or service
- Negotiating household chores
- Negotiating bedtime with your kids
- Arguing about politics or economics
- Discussing free will versus determinism
  …and much more…

The Argument occurs every time you try to convince someone else of your position or preference without using threats or force. **The Argument** lives in language every time you negotiate. **The Argument** comes to life every time you accept being rationally opposed without resorting to punishment, either directly or indirectly.

The Argument exists wherever people are willing to peacefully walk away from their disagreements. If you and the car dealer cannot agree on a price, nothing happens. He doesn't get your money; you don't get his car.

If, after **The Argument**, nothing happens, you know there has been an argument.

A hostage situation is not an argument, because if **The Argument** fails, violence follows. Violence is also used to initiate **The Argument**, in the form of kidnapping.

A husband willing to beat his wife for rejecting his preferences is not using **The Argument**, because violence follows a failure to comply.

A parent willing to hit her child if a disagreement continues is not using **The Argument**, because violence follows a failed negotiation.

A woman who pouts and withdraws emotionally if you don't do what she wants is not using **The Argument**, because she punishes you for non-compliance, rather than making a reasonable case for her preferences.

A Mafia shakedown is not an argument, because your store will be set on fire if you don't pay the protection money – violence follows rejection.

Taxation is not an argument, because you go to jail if you don't pay.

Do you see why I say that **The Argument** is civilization itself?

Civilization is the general agreement to *refrain from resorting to violence if negotiations fail*. Civilization manifests around those willing to reject violence if they are rejected.

We all have disagreements; that is natural and healthy. There are only two ways to resolve disagreements: through **The Argument**, or through the fist. Given that we are going to have endless disagreements, how do we want to resolve them?

One benefit of **The Argument** is that it reduces the prevalence of disagreements. If you are a car dealer and continually demand a million dollars for each of your beat-up old clunkers, all of your customers will disagree with you, so you must either adjust your price or go out of business.

Your wife tells you to wear a coat, but you don't think you need one. Every single time, you end up shivering with cold. At some point, hopefully, you will recognize that she is right and take your coat.

If, the first time your wife suggests you wear a coat because it is cold, you beat her, or scream at her, scaring her into not bringing the subject up again, you have not actually reduced the prevalence of disagreements, you have only driven those disagreements underground (and added a new one, which is her objection to your abuse).

On the other hand, using violence tends to escalate the prevalence of disagreements within society. If a business executive uses political connections to get a government subsidy, taxpayers will almost certainly disagree with that subsidy, which is why it needs to come from the government, rather than from voluntary investors. His competitors will also oppose it as well, and try to get a similar subsidy, which provokes even more competitors to do the same, provoking more resentment among taxpayers, and more sophistry from politicians and the media.

If government-protected unions and mandated minimum wages drive up the price of labor, this provokes unemployment, inflation and automation. Manufacturing jobs get shipped overseas, prices rise, and people get thrown out of work. This drives the need for unemployment insurance, welfare, retraining programs, you name it. In other words, one government program – raising wages – provokes an endless escalation of other government programs: rinse and repeat until bankruptcy.

Feast on the present; starve the future.

On the other hand, if a group of workers approach management with a list of demands – instead of running to the government – this is called **The Argument**. They want five dollars more an hour, and are willing to quit if they don't get it. The managers may agree, may disagree, may compromise – or may find some other solution - but the point is that *everyone is free to disagree*. If the negotiation fails, the workers may leave, the managers may quit, the business may be sold, who knows? And really, who cares, beyond the direct parties involved? The whole point is that it should remain an entirely voluntary and peaceful interaction.

If, however, the government throws the managers in jail, or fines them, or replaces them, then it is no longer an argument. It is a shakedown, pure and simple. The mafia with flags is still the mafia.

The Argument and Survival

Having to work for a living is not a shakedown, unless you view reality as a malevolent conspiracy. Life requires energy, and energy has to be provided or earned. The division of labor inherent in free-market negotiations is by far the most efficient way to create and provide the energy and materials required to live. It doesn't make sense for everyone to be a farmer; it makes sense for some people to specialize in medicine, and trade healthcare for other goods and/or services.

When you get hungry, or thirsty, or cold, no one is initiating force against you. Life is a process of self-generated and self-sustaining energy consumption, and you don't have the right to other people's energy, any more than you have a right to their time, or kidneys, or wallets, or children.

You may resent having to get out of bed and go to work, but resentment is not an argument. Resenting reality is one of the very definitions of immaturity. Growing up is learning not just to accept what you cannot change, but embrace it. Life requires energy; energy requires effort; expending effort is how you know you are alive: rocks and clouds and fossils are not so lucky.

The star-shreds that aggregated into the most improbable and miraculous explosion of your consciousness should be appreciated with more noble sentiments than resentment and depression.

THE ARGUMENT AS CIVILIZATION

In the hurly-burly of human interactions, we will always have disagreements, which is nothing to be upset about, as these productive conflicts produce the very sparks of progress. The fundamental question is: how will we resolve these disagreements? Historically, two "answers" have been implemented – fundamentalist religiosity, and government power. The third alternative – far more civilized – is **The Argument**, the reasoned debate, the honest willingness to submit to the higher standards of reason and evidence.

In the absence of this mutual surrender to a higher standard, we end up surrendering to lower standards – superstition, government force, bullying, intimidation, sophistry, you name it. In human society, it is literally **The Argument** – or else.

We all possess an animalistic side that seeks power over others, over resources. Curbing this side is the essential task of civilization, and the only tools it has at its disposal are philosophy, reason, evidence, and empiricism – the anti-madness magic of clear and critical thinking. We either surrender to facts, or we must be forced to surrender to each other. We are either dominated by reality, or by force and lies. As the old song says, you have to serve somebody.

Ostracism

But how do we deal with the anti-rational? It's all well and good to say we should submit to reason and evidence, but what happens to those who refuse?

Philosophical standards must be defended through *ostracism*. Intellectual ostracism, or refusing to engage with people who cannot rise to minimum standards of rationality, is an essential and often overlooked aspect of our society, and it pretty much runs everything, once you recognize it.

In a singing contest, bad singers are excluded from the contest; they are *ostracized*. Tennis championships work the same way. If you want a job, but don't get it, you are *ostracized* from your potential place of employment. If you ask a woman out on a date, and she says no, but you show up anyway, you are stalking her, i.e. not granting her the right to ostracize you. If you don't like going to a particular restaurant, you are *ostracizing* it. See how this works? By reading this, you are ostracizing all other books and activities. Ostracism is *everywhere*; it is far more prevalent than acceptance and engagement.

However, ostracism can provoke conflict. Rejecting people for not being up to scratch can make them quite upset, to say the least.

The decay of assertiveness in our intellectual classes is the fundamental undoing of our civilization. People who cannot argue, but keep trying, are like people who cannot sing, but keep trying. Given that we are all in a choir, so to speak, off-key singers destroy our collective harmony by being allowed to stay and wail.

Encouraging the incompetent to wage war in the realm of **The Argument** compromises the battle entirely.

The ancient enemy of philosophy – *sophistry*, or cunning rather than reasoning – is also the modern enemy of civilization. Those skilled in the dark arts of making the worse argument appear better are the counterfeiters of the true currency of reason. And, just as counterfeit money tends to drive real money out of circulation, bad arguments drive out good arguments, and we end up with political correctness and reactive hysteria rather than reasoned arguments from first principles.

There is an old saying, misattributed to Socrates, but nonetheless still very powerful: "When the debate is lost, slander becomes the tool of the loser."

A good singer cannot harmonize well with a bad singer. Pairing a poor singer with a good one does not simply diminish the good singer, it produces god-awful music.

Intellectual slander is the rage of those who wish to have the power to influence social discourse, but who lack the intellect, the training, the will or the maturity to productively engage in such debates. Many people at a rock concert would love to be the singer, or the guitarist, but they may lack the voice, the physical dexterity, or the sheer willpower to keep practising until their fingers bleed or they go hoarse. The ancient fable of the fox and the sour grapes holds true here: the fox who cannot reach the grapes storms off, telling himself that they were probably sour anyway and would taste terrible. What he cannot achieve, he attacks in order to minimize feelings of failure. He cannot satisfy his hunger through food, so he satisfies his rage through slander.

The bad singer who smashes his microphone, or who physically attacks other singers, has clearly lost the competition. However, if people are not trained in the discipline of rational argumentation, they cannot tell the difference between reasoning and manipulation, between truth and lies, between clear evidence and pretty stories. Those who wish to be paid for bad art must first blind the sensibilities of their audience.

The Argument and Charity

Let us suppose you get sick. If you are an adult, and of reasonable mental competence, you surely knew this was an inherent risk of being alive. The meaty machinery of mere existence is very messy and prone to failure.

Surely – at least in a free-market environment – you have bought insurance, so that your medical bills are covered. Alternatively, you could have saved your money, so that you can pay your bills directly.

One other option is to ask for charity.

All human desires are infinite, but all resources are finite. We all want to help others, but we do not want to be taken advantage of, or to subsidize – and thereby encourage – bad decisions.

It is merely a question of universality. Irresponsible people can only be subsidized by the responsible; spenders can only be rescued by the savers. If everyone is irresponsible, everyone loses. Thus responsibility must be a value. But if responsibility is a value, subsidizing – and thus rewarding – irresponsibility cannot also be a value.

People who have been raised badly can be forgiven one or two irresponsible decisions, just as someone learning a new language may occasionally say something inadvertently rude. However, continuing to subsidize people who continually make bad decisions is a very bad idea – it wastes precious and scarce social resources, and ends up punishing those making good decisions, while rewarding those making bad decisions, which is the exact opposite of how societies – as well as individuals – progress.

Those desiring charity must submit themselves to the discipline of those providing the charity, since requiring charity is very often a confession that you have made very bad decisions. Obviously, those who might give you charity want to be fairly sure that you are not going to continue to make those very bad decisions. This is both because they care about you, and also because few people will donate to a charity that does little more than subsidize and encourage irresponsibility. People donate to a charity because it is successful, i.e. it reduces the problems it is trying to address.

This is not at all the motive of those who run the welfare state – quite the opposite.

Pre-welfare state charities provided enough to live on, but would also involve themselves in your life, and they worked very hard to help you make better decisions. If you continually scorned them, and rejected their good advice, they would pull their resources back until you learned better. We give to charities to make people better, not worse.

This form of benevolent control can be a great sting to the ego of the incompetent, but that is necessary and helpful for everyone involved.

Charity is part of **The Argument**, because it remains a voluntary negotiation: both parties can walk away without resorting to violence. If you want charity, it may come with conditions – that is part of the negotiation. If you find the charitable conditions not to your liking, you can either forgo the charity, or get charity from someone else whose conditions are more to your liking.

Charity and the Division of Kindness

Another possibility exists – or at least used to – which is the *division of kindness*. This is not the same as direct charity, but represents an accumulation of voluntary social indebtedness.

Imagine a street with a kindly spinster named Elizabeth – unmarried but big-hearted – who organizes games for children, makes them snacks, babysits for little or no money, volunteers to help people, brings food to the sick and visits the elderly.

This kindness is wonderful and deeply inspiring to behold, and it is of great value to the entire community. Elizabeth provides an essential glue that holds everyone together.

Of course, all the time Elizabeth spends being kind and generous is time she is *not* spending making money. So, she ends up poor, but with great credit in the infinite bank of social exchanges.

After years of kindness, Elizabeth may fall ill, or be in danger of losing her house, or simply have a great desire to see Alaska before she dies. Innately recognizing the great debt they owe her, her neighbours may very well decide to pay for her treatment, or save her house, or fund her cruise. Her help along the way has allowed her neighbours to focus more on making money. They have more money because Elizabeth was more kind. When she is in need, they can take some of the excess money her kindness helped them to make, and return it to her.

This is not exactly charity, since Elizabeth's kindness within the community was not exactly charity to begin with. Furthermore, if we assume that she is much better at being kind than making money – while others in the neighborhood are better at making money than being kind – then we can label this the *division of kindness*. This form of a largely cashless economy is how neighborhoods used to function, as did marriages and the raising of children.

Mothers used to stay home and invest countless hours raising their children. In return, their adult children would take care of them when the parents got old.

Wives used to stay home. Husbands used to make money and share it with their wives. Was this charity? Of course not, because wives were running a household and raising children, which is perhaps the most essential service in the human economy. For, without this service none of us would be here to make money in the fading remnants of the free market.

Even child-raising has elements of the *division of kindness*. Parents who keep their promises to their children have every right to expect their children to keep their word in return. Parents who respect their children have every right to expect reciprocal respect. Bestowing kindness grants us the right to expect kindness. Children are largely raised to be moral through the imprinting of their parents' good behavior and through the rational expectation of reciprocity for virtue.

The vast majority of human interactions fall into this non-cash benevolence economy, and our failure to recognize this is threatening civilization itself. We are increasingly substituting state power for **The Argument**.

Charity and Punishment

Those in a free society who make bad decisions, and will not mend their ways, should not be helped anymore, at least above a bare minimum.

It is the *voluntary* nature of charity that gives it its peculiar power to improve both individuals and societies. As mentioned above, arguments without negative repercussions are worse than useless; they discredit civilization as a whole.

If you cannot be fired, you tend not to work hard. If you suffer few if any negative consequences for bad decisions, you tend not to make better decisions. Sparks fly from the sharpening of the blade.

It is no accident that many university professors have tenure – they basically cannot be fired – and very easy work weeks, months off in the summer, six-figure salaries, regular sabbaticals, conferences in exotic places, huge pensions and benefits, and other such tasty goodies. In a truly free market, would there be people who work longer hours for less pay to taste the deep pleasures of instructing young and eager minds? I'm sure there would be, but universities do not operate in a free-market environment. Government accreditation and grants, unions and subsidized student loans all dissolve market discipline.

Teachers and professors are not paid by **The Argument** – is it any wonder that they scorn and attack the free market, voluntary interactions – and free speech, so often?

Voluntary charity is an essential part of **The Argument**. And remember, **The Argument** is defined by the ability to leave the negotiation without violence.

The government welfare state is not part of **The Argument**, since you cannot leave the negotiation or refuse to contribute to the wealth transfer. If you don't pay your taxes, at some point you will most likely stare right down the barrel of state power.

This is the price we face for abandoning **The Argument** in favor of force. We no longer help the poor, but rather entrap them. We no longer coach people out of making bad decisions; we subsidize even worse decisions. The poor do not always have to be with us, *contra* Jesus, but they sure as hell will be as long as we avoid **The Argument** in favor of the state.

THE ARGUMENT AND PARENTING

*T**he Argument*** is often considered to be for adults only, inaccessible to mere children, who are believed to be pre-rational.

Nothing could be further from the truth, or more conducive to the spread of anti-rationality.

Studies have shown that infants are able to perform mathematical reasoning at the age of *eight months*, and they begin moral reasoning at only three months of age! Children are capable of rationality – and in particular, moral reasoning – just as they are capable of trading to mutual benefit, as anyone who has seen a gaggle of children haggling over Halloween candy can confirm.

Children are born negotiators, since negotiation often begins from a state of dependency, or physical weakness. The man who is losing often begs for clemency and promises benefits for mercy. The negotiation begins in defeat; the victor rarely needs to initiate it.

Young children generally cannot achieve their goals directly, and so need to negotiate. Depending on the receptivity and rationality of parents, childhood negotiation tactics can include whining, temper tantrums, complaining, being negative, offering rewards, promising good behavior and so on. These are opening salvos of a negotiation designed to encourage – or discourage – parental choice to conform to the child's desires.

As adults, we generally don't think that violence is a good way to solve problems. Somehow, though, for many parents hitting children seems like a *great* idea.

Hitting children merely instructs them in the principle that *might makes right*; that the bigger person willing to use violence always gets his or her way, and that fear of punishment, and not love of virtue, should be one's guiding principle in life.

When you see a society that rejects **The Argument**, you see a society that substitutes force and/or abuse in place of negotiation. When you look at such a society, what you are really seeing is a society that has used force and/or abuse to raise its children.

Children bond with, and morally justify, whoever raises them. If they are raised in the shadows of authoritarian violence, they will not consider a dictatorship immoral. Asking a child to respect liberty when he was raised coercively is like asking a child to understand Japanese, when he has been raised speaking only English.

To some degree, children are clay when they are young; they harden as they age.

Some countries have substituted neglect for direct abuse – the daycare generation – which has arguably had even more negative effects.

This is why I speak so often and passionately about the concept of peaceful parenting, because I want a free and peaceful world. How you teach children to resolve disputes becomes their default position when they become adults. If you use violence to resolve disputes (which resolves nothing, of course, but merely breeds temporary and resentful compliance) then your children will grow up running to the government, giving up their hard-won liberties, whenever social conflicts arise.

Those who reject **The Argument** were themselves rejected as children.

THE ETYMOLOGY OF THE ARGUMENT

The Argument began in ancient Greece, and was primarily associated with Socrates. The Socratic method is a way of probing abstract statements, particularly about morality, in order to determine if they hold true under most reasonable circumstances.

This was the first real counterattack in the mostly endless war that reason wages against sophistry. **The Argument** engages the prefrontal cortex, the seat of reasoning in the brain. Sophistry attempts to bypass the prefrontal cortex and activate the amygdala, the seat of hyper-emotional "fight or flight" reactions.

The philosopher engages your intellect. The sophist provokes an emotional response in order to bypass your intellect. The philosopher makes the moral case for a just war, if such a case can indeed be made. The sophist tells you that you will die if war is not started.

The philosopher patiently makes the case, through reason and evidence. The sophist appeals to fear, anger, horror and sentimentality in order to threaten you with ostracism if you do not obey his commandments. If you disagree with the philosopher, you are welcome to engage or leave as you see fit. If you disagree with the sophist – at least about anything he considers important – you are attacked and smeared.

The philosopher lives in the realm of *positive economics*, offering reason and evidence as a methodology for pursuing truth. Truth is the goal of the philosopher's *truth arguments*; virtue is the goal of his *value arguments*. He combines the two to produce *happiness*: reason leads to virtue leads to happiness.

The sophist is the chief demon in the living hell of *negative economics*. If you submit to him, he will refrain from destroying your reputation. The philosopher offers a positive; the sophist offers to avoid inflicting a negative. The philosopher does not provoke fear, or threaten you with negative consequences, or punish those who disagree. The sophist is a monster of intimidation, more than willing to follow the ancient tribal model of rewarding his friends and punishing his enemies.

Socrates was a philosopher; most gods are sophists.

John Stuart Mill was a philosopher; governments are sophists.

Aristotle was a philosopher; the media are sophists.

Which are you?

OSTRACISM VERSUS PUNISHMENT

When I say that the philosopher does not punish you, I do not mean that your level of rationality has no effect on his responses. The philosopher will studiously avoid privately engaging with antirational individuals, in the same way that he avoids doing business with a known counterfeiter, since all such interaction merely legitimizes the ignorant and corrupt. I don't pretend to play tennis with someone who shows up with a hockey stick and a broken flashlight.

Public debates are another matter entirely. Engaging with antirational individuals in a public forum can be wonderfully instructive to the audience – especially now, in the age of the Internet – when the audience can easily run into the many millions.

A philosopher enters a debate with the assumption that his partner respects reason and evidence. If you reject reason, you waste a philosopher's time, and he will not likely give you more of it, just as a cook won't give you another serving if you keep throwing his food into the garbage. The philosopher may also encourage other people to not waste their time on you, which may have the effect of removing you from public forums and debate platforms. This may seem shocking to some, but it is no different from what we all did as children, when a particular playmate would break the rules, or whine, or play too violently. He would not be invited next time, at least until he reformed his bad behavior.

This form of ostracism is not an act of aggression, but rather of exclusivity. If you don't let everyone in the neighborhood use your car, you are not stealing from them; rather, you assert the exclusive use of your own property. Kissing a woman against her will is never the moral equivalent of the woman who decides not to go out with you. The first example initiates aggression; the second asserts her right to the exclusive use of herself.

People often complain about the ostracism that can result from public displays of immaturity, as if it was some form of censorship or aggression. This is little more than verbal abuse used to avoid the negative consequences of one's own bad behavior (and it is viewed by even the remotely wise as an extension of the bad behavior that earned the ostracism in the first place)!

If you heap verbal abuse on an acquaintance, and that acquaintance no longer wishes to be associated with you, calling him a "censorious fascist" is merely a continuation of the abuse that severed the potential friendship in the first place. This type of retaliatory behaviour is actually a subtle signal sent out to draw in other bad actors and enlist their support. The resulting feeding frenzy of verbal abuse and public smearing should make it clear to everyone *exactly* who the bad actors are. But unfortunately, this rarely happens.

When the sophist sharks attack the innocent – the moral, in general – people often back away, for fear of being bitten in the same way. This momentary appeasement may save the day, but loses the future; it merely reinforces the successful social strategy of attacking someone whose integrity caused you to humiliate yourself. You may save yourself in the moment, but the sharks only grow stronger and breed.

THE ARGUMENT AND ENFORCEMENT

Society has rules, some good, some bad, because no society can oper-ate without rules. A central philosophical question is: how are these rules to be justified and enforced?

If the philosopher fails to answer this question – or if his answer is rejected by society – then there is, extraordinarily rapidly, no such thing as society anymore.

Society is an aggregation of self-chosen interactions. Where people are *forced* to live in proximity, they are no longer a society, any more than animals in a zoo can be considered a natural ecosystem, or cellmates can be considered roommates.

Rational social rules work best when they are accepted by the vast major-ity (it would be best if everyone accepted them, but that is unrealistic), and in particular when those social rules are voluntarily obeyed through moral self-restraint. A free society can deal with a small number of rule-breakers. When the number of those who disobey reasonable social rules grows too large, society breaks down.

Thus, the primary job of the philosopher is to make social rules rational and comprehensible, offer up a strong case for the rewards of following them, and encourage ostracism against those who repeatedly break those rules.

When ostracism is used to punish those who break social rules, *nothing more needs to be done*: that is the simple beauty of ostracism. If you find someone unpleasant or offensive, disassociate from him. If the contents of a magazine are upsetting to you, don't lift a finger to pay for it, either directly or indirectly, through advertising on the web. If you have a bad date with a woman, don't call her again: nothing could be easier. Inaction as social enforcement! You can contribute to virtue by having a nap.

Civility breaks down – society and civilization itself breaks down – when ostracism is thwarted. All moral rules require a carrot and a stick, because people can be guaranteed to respond to incentives far more than they respond to moral ideals.

Where ostracism is thwarted, the value of **The Argument** diminishes.

When I was a kid, science teachers used to play the occasional video in the classroom, and the first question we all asked was, "Will this be on the test?"

If the answer was "no," the necessity of paying attention was diminished.

The question that was really being asked was not whether the video material would be on the test, but rather: *will I suffer any negative consequences for not paying attention?*

It works the same way with social rules. However much we might be inspired by moral abstractions and virtuous ideals, we remain, as King Lear screamed at the wind, "bare forked animals." Most people seek to gain the greatest amount of resources with the least amount of effort. People who win the lottery usually quit their jobs. Our internal algorithms for re-source optimization are constantly probing the question: *will I suffer any negative consequences for not obeying these rules?*

Will this be on the test?

Businesses that woo potential customers must provide continual value. The quality of organizations that do *not* have to woo inevitably degrades. One need only look at the differences in efficiency between a capitalist factory and a communist factory to understand this. If the free-market factory fails to provide value, the company goes out of business and its resources are released for use elsewhere. If a communist factory fails to provide value, it does not go out of business; it just lurches on, zombie-like, until the entire system collapses. As the old saying went in the Soviet Union, "They pretend to pay us, and we pretend to work."

How do you get the best people to work for you? As an employer, you have to offer benefits, flexibility, higher salary and other perks. How do you get hired in the free-market? By offering more value to your employer than you will consume in salary and expenses.

A free society offers the benefits of voluntary cooperation and interaction, and the significant penalty called ostracism. A waiter who pleases his customers keeps his job; a waiter who spits in the soup does not. A business owner protects the value of his business by exercising ostracism against inefficient employees. Marital partners generally promise monogamy, thus ostracizing for all time future alternative sexual partners. A cabbie does not generally pick up other customers while you are sitting in his cab: you have paid for his *ostracism of other potential customers* for the duration of your trip. When you pay for a hotel room, you generally do not wake up with a stranger in the next bed (Aerosmith excluded). You pay for exclusive use, or the ostracism of other potential guests in your hotel room.

Societies that encourage ostracism flourish, because their social rules contain rewards and punishments. Societies that disallow or punish ostracism lower – and eventually destroy – the value of **The Argument**, because failure to conform to **The Argument** no longer carries penalties.

For instance, through the mechanism of the welfare state, you are forced to subsidize the poor. You are not allowed to ostracize those whose poverty is the result of their own decisions (an ostracism that could actually help them by providing highly motivational negative feedback).

There are poor people who need and deserve charity and help, but there are also poor people whose lives are further destroyed through charity and help. Giving money to people whose poverty results from bad decisions only pays them to make more bad decisions, as we can see from the proliferation of single motherhood.

Societies that lose the capacity to ostracize people who make terrible decisions (and thereby lose the capacity to benevolently guide them), also lose control over the value of social rules, and thus become progressively more indebted, totalitarian and censorious, because the only way to punish people when ostracism is outlawed is through the verbal abuse of the sophists and the legal force of the state.

If a man goes broke because he is a drunkard or a compulsive gambler, giving him unconditional money feeds his addiction. A benevolent soul would sit down with him and demand, as a condition of charity, that he seek treatment for his bad behavior. In other words, true charity would make an argument for what he *should do*, with the reward of money, and the punishment of ostracism, as the conditions. Arguments with neither benefits nor punishments are fairly useless noises, arid intellectual exercises without enforcement mechanisms. They inhabit the useless cloud pillar of ivory tower abstractions, looking progressively more ridiculous and futile as time marches on.

When negative consequences are removed, the value of **The Argument** is diminished. We may say to a single mother who continues to have children out of wedlock, that she is morally wrong for doing so, because children who grow up without fathers are damaged by paternal absence. But she may just laugh in our faces, because she gets money from the government anyway. It's hard to get people's attention when you have neither positive nor negative consequences to offer them. If you've just bought the car, it's hard to maintain the salesman's attention. You get the idea…

The welfare state allows us to safely make fun of moralists (for a time, anyway).

For arguments to gain traction, they must be arguments *for* and/or *against* something. Arguments that do not benefit, or help avoid disaster, are foolish exercises in linguistic futility. The old argument that a woman should wait until marriage before having children carried weight, because the negative consequences of single motherhood were so disastrous to her – and her immediate family (at least before the advent of the welfare state).

A woman who understands the negative consequences of single motherhood – for herself, for her children, and for society at large – and who wishes the best for everyone involved, will simply not become a single mother. Thus, no arguments are needed for a woman with knowledge and a commitment to virtue.

Who Are Arguments For?

So – who are arguments for? Who is the target audience or demographic for arguments?

When you argue against single motherhood, for instance, what are your arguments?

We do not need much theorizing over this question, because – again, prior to the welfare state – the arguments were very common and deeply rooted in social standards. You should not become a single mother because doing so results in ostracism from men seeking marriage partners. There are other factors, of course, such as family honor and fidelity to religious dictates, but once the welfare state came into the picture, most of these arguments fell away, so they cannot be considered essential.

If you are a single mother, and will be ostracized by men who want to get married, then who will pay your bills? Children can be expensive, and paying for childcare generally cancels out the value of a single mother's pay check. So, the single mom generally ends up living with her parents, who have to pay her bills. This massive negative consequence was the spur that impelled the social ostracism of single mothers. (By the way, this ostracism also improved the outlook for the children of single mothers, who were generally given up for adoption to stable two-parent families, and had significantly better lives thereby.)

In this way, **The Argument** against single motherhood had some teeth, so to speak – potential ostracism was a warning against the negative consequences that directly manifested within society. Since single mothers had no mechanism by which to compel responsible taxpayers to pay for their children, they had little choice but to give them up for adoption, or find other methods of dealing with the problem, such as pretending that the newborn was actually the child of the mother's married mother.

These days, arguing against single motherhood will often get you branded as some sort of hateful misogynist. Now that there are no longer any direct negative costs to single motherhood, only a nasty person would criticize single mothers. In the case of single motherhood, this also shows how little society is motivated by compassion and care for the future of children (as if the national debt was not example enough of that!).

The rise of the welfare state coincided with the rise of political correctness. When negative consequences for bad decisions are removed, information is inevitably repressed. The welfare state subsidized the rise of single motherhood, which created a strong constituency opposed to information revealing the negative effects on children of single mothers, which created a phalanx of pseudo-intellectuals who protected single mothers – and society – from basic facts.

Do you see the pattern? When direct negative consequences are removed, arguments against negative behaviors come to be treated as irrational prejudice. Arguments are no longer positive cases against negative outcomes, but a species of emotional bigotry.

THE AUDIENCE AND THE ARGUMENT

Now we approach one of the most fundamental questions of **The Argument** – who is its intended audience?

The simple answer is, of course, *everyone* – *everyone* benefits from **The Argument**, even if they don't participate in **The Argument**. Even if you just passively listen to an argument, your mind is improved; your mental health is enhanced; and your ability to reason is advanced through exposure.

We all suffer from confirmation bias – and the word "suffer" itself is a kind of confirmation bias – since confirmation bias is what enables continuity in culture and moral standards and social rules. Each of us is invested in our belief systems, just as we are invested in our children, our marriages and our careers. We should not give them up lightly. Confirmation bias is the wall that protects hard-won and long-lasting social values; it is the immune system that helps protect values from sophistry. (Naturally, confirmation bias has its well-known dark side, but it is important to remember the case *for* confirmation bias as well.)

When you are right, confirmation bias is a virtue.

Those willing to subjugate their egos to reality know the benefits of **The Argument**, and do not need the threat of punishment or the bribery of approval to pursue the rewards of rigorous rational verbal combat.

Those unwilling to subjugate their egos to reality do not benefit from **The Argument**: it hardens their belief systems into irrational dogma. They need a stick rather than a carrot to conform to the requirements of **The Argument**.

Think of a tennis game. Watching an expert tennis player gives average tennis players something to aim for and also helps maintain their humility. Whenever we apply ourselves to a particular task, we are all experts relative to yesterday – merely looking behind us, at our wake, makes us feel that we have achieved more than we have. Looking ahead, to those with a true mastery of the task, reminds us how far we have to go, which can be painful, but also spurs ambition and dedication.

What attitude should expert tennis players have towards those with no desire to play by the rules? If you want three serves instead of two, or to win a tie game by one point instead of two, or to demand the expanded lines of the doubles court for a singles match, how should an expert tennis player respond?

And here, inevitably, we return to the issue of ostracism.

Expert tennis players know that if you want to play tennis, you have to play by the rules. If you want to regularly break the rules of tennis, you might become good at some kind of game, but that game is definitely *not* tennis. Training to become good at cheating at tennis is training to become bad at real tennis.

The requirements of tennis are simple – get the ball over the net and keep it in bounds. Following these rules does not mean you will win, but it does mean that you get to stay in the game. The requirements of **The Argument** are also simple: stick to reason and evidence. This is the "necessary but not sufficient" requirement for participation in **The Argument** – it does not mean you will win, but you get to play.

Of course, seeing when a ball is out of bounds is far easier than seeing when sophistry, unreason, counter-empiricism and manipulation muck up **The Argument**. But that is why *this* book is so important!

If you want to cheat at tennis, and an expert tennis player no longer wants to play with you, your fragile ego will probably lash out, calling him "too rigid," "hung up on details," or a bully seeking to impose his arbitrary will on you, and so on.

In the same way, if you want to cheat at **The Argument**, and an expert debater no longer wants to argue with you, your fragile ego will probably lash out, claiming victory, taunting weakness on the part of your former opponent, and crowing that all who wish to avoid you have in fact been defeated by you. To the uneducated masses, this strategy may work (another reason why I wrote this book).

If we wish to maintain the rules of tennis – or chess, or debates, or civilizations – experts *must* ostracize those who refuse to play by the rules. Rejecting incompetence – in any structured interaction, incompetence is in fact *anti*-competence – is essential to maintaining basic civilized standards.

If we want to maintain a civilization, we must defend **The Argument** at all costs.

The incompetent will naturally rail against the supposed "injustice" and "intolerance" of this ostracism, because they want to play the game with the rules tilted in their favor. While wildly wrong, this is natural. The stakes of controlling **The Argument** are the highest possible in society, and a trillion-dollar prize can be understood to carry with it a strong impulse to tilt the playing field.

Ostracizing the incompetent from **The Argument** also serves to create two sub-societies within the larger society: the society of those who respect **The Argument**, and the society of those who do not. Given that **The Argument** as a whole rests upon empiricism, having these two opposing epistemological methodologies in society can be enormously instructive. Place a conceptual wall between these two opposing camps, and see which one does better over time, and which does worse. Where reason fails, empiricism instructs (often brutally, but that is why we respect reason as a shield against the ugly blowback of the consequences of rejecting reason. See: Venezuela).

Fundamentally, **The Argument** has two customers: those who use **The Argument** like a man trying to reach a roof uses a ladder, and those who use **The Argument** like a pickpocket uses the distraction of bumping into you to steal your wallet. The former need no punishment, since they use **The Argument** as the primary tool in their pursuit of truth, integrity, and virtue. The latter need the punishment of ostracism, just as someone who urinates in your swimming pool needs to find another place to swim.

THE ARGUMENT AND REALITY

Our minds are capable of error, which is the greatest strength and weakness of the human condition. Most organisms react automatically or instinctually to environmental cues: the lion is hungry, it chases a gazelle; the gazelle is frightened, it runs away; the rabbit is horny, it makes more rabbits.

This automatic input–output mechanism has little room for error, and thus little room for experimentation and improvement. The human mind has the capacity to rise above – and often below – mere empirical sense data. Because we can reject the evidence of our direct senses, we get all the glories of science, and all the terrors of superstition. The sun and moon appear the same size to us; we can discover that they are different, in reality. The world looks largely flat; we can ascertain that it is not. We also fear the wrath of those long dead, and because their personalities live on in our minds, we imagine them stalking our hallways with wet chains and staring eyes.

We gain reason and science by using the direct evidence of our senses to extrapolate and discover general rules, which we can then apply to contradict the direct evidence of our senses. The stability and predictability of matter and energy create within us the capacity for empirical rationality. In other words, concepts are valid because atoms and physical laws exist, and are predictable. Water exists because the atomic aggregation of H^2O

has stable properties and characteristics. Water below 0°C turns into ice because it possesses stable properties and characteristics.

Our most abstract concepts are built on the properties of invisible rules and atoms, just as the glow of a city is visible from space, while its inhabitants are not.

Our capacity to extract and conceptualize physical properties into conceptual patterns is unique in the animal kingdom: it is how we can reliably send a probe past Jupiter.

Reason is our codification of rules found in nature. Aristotle's three laws of logic directly correspond to the kind of sense perception worked through by every growing baby. An object is itself and nothing else; an object is either itself or something else; an object must be either itself or something else. A ball is a ball; a ball is either a ball or something else; an object must be either a ball or something else. This is a description of stable physical properties over time. A ball rolled behind the couch does not suddenly become part of the couch – this is the development of *object constancy*. You reach behind the couch to get the ball, which is still there. Toddlers will reach into a glass of water to retrieve a ball dropped therein; they will not reach into retrieve milk that is poured into the same glass of water, because they understand that the milk has been mixed into the water and cannot be retrieved.

The stable, consistent and predictable behavior of matter and energy gives rise to the requirement for stable, consistent and predictable patterns of thought – necessary for us to say anything valid about reality. There is no such thing as a cold candle flame. Thus if I say that candle flames are cold to the touch, I am incorrect. If I have a scientific hypothesis that requires a candle flame to be cold to the touch, there is no point testing it, because my initial premise is anti-empirical. If I have a scientific hypothesis that requires candle flames to be simultaneously both cold and hot to the touch, I don't need to know anything about candle flames to reject the hypothesis, because it is self-contradictory in its inception. In the same way, if I start an argument by stating that for my conclusion to be true, gravity must both attract and repel matter simultaneously, no testing or further analysis is required: my theory contradicts itself at its root, and can be dismissed without further inquiry.

This works equally well with concepts. There is no such thing as a "square circle," and if my argument requires the existence of such a self-contradictory concept, it can be dismissed without further inquiry. It disproves itself in the contradiction of the definition.

This is why **The Argument** first requires logical consistency, and only then empirical verification.

This requirement exists because **The Argument** attempts to say something valid or true about rational empirical reality, and thus must conform to the requirements of truth.

THE ARGUMENT AND TRUTH

When we wish to say something true about reality, what we say must be rational, because reality is rational.

When we wish to say something true about reality, what we say must be consistent, because reality is consistent.

Truth is in general a word that means "a rational statement about empirical reality that can be objectively verified."

If I say that an apple is green, this can be objectively verified: even if you are color-blind, you can check the wavelength bouncing off the apple and see if it falls into the category of "green."

If I say that gases expand when heated, this can be objectively verified. If I say that objects fall to earth at 9.8 m/s per second, this can be objectively verified.

If my argument requires contradictory states, no disproof is needed: the disproof is built into the contradictory definition. If I say that objects simultaneously accelerate toward and away from Earth at 9.8 m/s per second, no one needs to go and empirically test my statement. If I say that a tomato is all red and all black at the same time, you don't need to go and check every tomato in the universe to invalidate my statement.

If I provide a mathematical "proof" that requires 2+2 to equal both 4 and 5 at the same time, no further investigation is required to invalidate my proposition.

THE ARGUMENT AND EXISTENCE

When it comes to proposing the existence of things, there are three categories:

1. Things that exist
2. Things that *could* exist, and
3. Things that *cannot* exist.

Birds exist; unicorns *could* exist; square circles *cannot* exist.

Lizards exist; flying lizards could exist (and did!); magical dragons cannot exist.

Definitions matter, as we will see shortly. If I define a unicorn as a horse with a horn on its head, such an animal *could* exist somewhere in the universe, perhaps even in some hidden place on Earth. However, if I define a unicorn as a magical horse that can fly without wings and is shrouded in fire and ice simultaneously, we do not need to examine the universe from end to end to discover if such an impossible creature could exist. Self-consistent entities may exist; self-contradictory entities may not exist. Or, if you prefer, they do not exist.

Consistency with categories is also essential for a successful argument. If I define mammals as warm-blooded creatures with hair, I cannot arbitrarily throw a single blue lizard into the mix and call it a mammal, for the simple reason that it is hairless and cold-blooded, and thus does not conform to the definition of "mammal."

The reason for this is, of course, that concepts *describe* reality; they do not *alter* it. If I whisper the word "mammal" to my blue lizard, the word does not change its physiology, or the temperature of its blood, or whether it has mammary glands. Definitions *describe* reality; they are the conceptual shadows cast by objects, and shadows have no capacity to change the shape of the objects that cast them.

In other words, concepts are *passive*, not active. They describe real categories; they cannot define them solely through language. If you understand this, you are well on your way to mastering **The Argument**.

Thus, if I want to say something that is *true*, what I say needs to be rational and consistent. This requirement is a bare minimum – rationality and consistency are merely the tickets that get you into **The Argument**. They do not guarantee that you will win **The Argument**, but they do help you lose with dignity – and indeed profit – should such be the outcome.

To fully grasp this, imagine me having a debate with someone about whether I dreamt of an elephant on September 24 of last year. It is clear that no such debate could ever be resolved to anyone's satisfaction, since what I'm describing could never be verified empirically. Maybe I dreamt about an elephant, maybe I didn't. Maybe I sincerely *believe* that I dreamt about an elephant that night and could even pass a lie detector test. But perhaps I am mistaken: it was the night before, or was something that looked a little bit like an elephant, but had flaming wings, which could not be rationally classified as an elephant. The list of problems could be virtually endless.

How would you respond to an invitation to such a debate? If I asked you to publicly debate me on this most pressing question, what would you say?

Surely, you would say that there is nothing to debate.

And, of course, you would be entirely right.

What if the debate topic was: *was it **possible** that Stefan Molyneux dreamt of an elephant on September 24 of last year?*

Again, you would say that there was nothing to debate: of course it was *possible* that I dreamt about an elephant on that night – but so what?

What if the debate topic was: *was it possible that Stefan Molyneux turned **into** an elephant on September 24 of last year?*

You would say: is there really anything to debate? Even if I insisted that this impossible transformation occurred, it would be relatively simple to disprove, just by having me walk out onto the debate stage without a trunk.

(And even if an elephant *did* enter the debate stage, who could possibly know if it was once me?)

THE ARGUMENT AND EMPIRICISM

We have talked about the relationship of **The Argument** to empiricism, or objective sense data verification – are there arguments unrelated to empiricism? In other words, are there abstract arguments that never overlap or impact on objective, empirical reality?

I would say that there are, in the same way that there can be Klingon or wood elf biology – such abstract "disciplines" can exist, but so what? We can certainly design arguments and abstractions that never overlap or impact on empirical reality, but that is like spending weeks developing a business plan for an imaginary product in an alternate dimension.

Does it make any sense to propose an argument for the best way to structure and organize society, with no reference whatsoever to any empirical evidence? Can we say that the free market is better, or that communism is better, or that democratic socialism is better, merely by debating abstractions – or does the accumulated historical evidence for a variety of approaches matter?

The essence of philosophy is morality – since that is the one area that nothing else can touch directly – and morality refers to actions in the real world. Thoughts can be right or wrong, valid or invalid, correct or incorrect – but only actions can be good or evil. There is no such thing as "*thought crime.*" Morality relates to *universally preferable behavior*, just as medicine relates to measurable physical properties and states in the body. Discussing merely abstract philosophy might be a fun intellectual exercise or hobby, but it is little more than playing scales on the piano – good for practice, bad for a concert hall. Playing scales is not the same as making music – music is the empirical effect of practice. Rational consistency is not the same as making an argument – consistency is the practice, **The Argument** is the effect.

One can imagine going to a medical conference and talking about imaginary cures for imaginary diseases, but if none of that arid intellectualism impacted the behaviour or practice of any doctors in the real world, let's just say it would be a pretty sparsely attended lecture. Arguments change behaviours, behaviours are empirical.

The Argument cannot be separated from empiricism, since the consistency and predictability of empirical matter is what gives **The Argument** its structure, providing its requirement for rational consistency. The structure and properties of **The Argument** are directly derived from the structure and properties of empirical reality, and so even if an argument has no effect on empirical reality, it is still derived from empirical reality.

Thus **The Argument** is not designed to change minds, but rather to change *behavior*. A dietitian is not primarily trying to change your mind, but your eating habits. Changing your mind is necessary, but not sufficient. A piano teacher is not trying to get you to practice, but to improve your playing – practising is necessary, but not sufficient.

A moralist – a philosopher – is not trying to change your mind, but your behaviour. He is trying to stimulate your moral courage, or integrity, or consistency – to provoke behavioral changes of some kind.

If you doubt this, I challenge you to imagine an argument that produces no changed behaviors whatsoever. All arguments are arguments for empirical action.

The Argument without empiricism is *not* *The Argument*.

THE ESSENTIAL ELEMENTS OF THE ARGUMENT

These are the essential elements of *The Argument*:

1. It must be a rational proposition, consistent with itself and empirical reality.
2. It must make claims about empirical, testable reality.
3. It must contain a *null hypothesis*. In other words, there must be some standard by which it could potentially be disproven (this distinguishes *The Argument* from a mere empty assertion).
4. Its terms must be objectively definable, to the satisfaction of both parties (if definitions cannot be agreed upon, no productive debate can ensue).
5. Both parties must agree to abide by reason and evidence, at the expense of their own propositions.

The analogy to tennis rules may be helpful:

1. Tennis must have rational, self-consistent rules.
2. Tennis rules must be empirical and testable.
3. Conversely, there must be an empirical and testable methodology for knowing if someone has broken the rules of tennis.
4. Tennis rules must be objectively definable, to the satisfaction of both parties.

5. Both parties must agree to abide by these rational, objective and consistent rules, even at the expense of their own victory, for the simple reason that victory is defined by the rules, not by the individual's desire for victory, which is assumed.

It is clear that the game of tennis only exists because it satisfies the above requirements, and it is also clear that victory cannot be achieved in opposition to these requirements. If one player thinks he gets three serves, while the other player knows he only gets two, the game cannot continue until this discrepancy is resolved.

Tennis rules are arbitrary, at least to some degree. There is no objective, rational empirical reason why a player gets only two serves instead of three (and don't even get me started on the arbitrariness of *Love – 15 – 30 – 40 – Advantage*), so in this case, you look up the rules in an official book.

When I was seven, I planned an entire chess gambit against my brother based on the understanding that my King could move two spaces at once. When the time came for my checkmate move, I was informed that my King could only move *one* space at a time. I strenuously resisted this proposition, until an encyclopedia the size of a Hogwarts spell book was taken down from a shelf, and I saw the rules in black and white, and had to withdraw my move. My tears – quite rightly – changed nothing.

Here we can see an example of a standard that is empirically verifiable – not with reference to the physical properties of matter – but rather with reference to the established rules of the game.

The Argument is the chess game of society, and victory is civilization.

THE ARGUMENT AND RIGHTS

Many political arguments take the form of claiming that a certain benefit is a "human right."

It is a "human right" to be educated, to receive healthcare, to achieve egalitarian outcomes relative to other groups, and so on.

The challenge here is that any characteristic of human beings must apply to *all* human beings, not just some human beings. It also must exist contemporaneously, or for all human beings at the same time. The characteristic of mammals called "mammary glands" applies to all mammals, and not only to some mammals. All mammals can have mammary glands contemporaneously, or at the same time. One mammal does not possess breasts at the expense of another.

When one animal achieves a value at the expense of another animal, this is called predation, or parasitism. A lion achieves life at the expense of the life of its prey.

Characteristics of matter such as inertia and gravity must apply to all matter, not just to some matter. These characteristics must also exist contemporaneously; in other words, all mass must possess these characteristics at the same time.

If it is a "human right" to be educated, then this cannot apply to *all* human beings, since some people must be in the process of being educated, while others are in the process of educating them. In the same way, this right cannot exist contemporaneously, for all human beings at the same time, for the same reason.

(Also, the "right to be educated" is indefinable: educated in what? For how long? To what degree? These questions cannot be objectively defined or answered, like all questions of "degree." Let's say that 12 years of education is a human right: why 12 and not 13, or 12 minus one minute?)

In other words, the "human right" to be educated is a right possessed by some at the expense of the rights possessed by others. Two people cannot be simultaneously educating each other at the same time. One person cannot both be a teacher and student at the same time.

Thus, education cannot be a *human* right, any more than healthcare or housing or egalitarian outcomes.

Syllogistically, **The Argument** looks like this:

1. All human beings have the right to "X"
2. Some human beings must provide "X"
3. Those who must provide "X" cannot simultaneously receive "X"
4. Therefore not all human beings can have the right to "X"

Self-ownership, on the other hand, can be exercised by all human beings at the same time, and can exist contemporaneously, and thus could be considered at least a property of humanity, rather than a "right," which is, to put it mildly, somewhat of a challenging concept in the realm of rationality.

DEFINING DEFINITIONS

The art of **The Argument** lies essentially in the question of definitions.

It is not only an amateur mistake to avoid defining terms – it is an anti-rational mistake. (Calling it a "mistake" is the kindest word I can think of, but it is seldom that innocent.)

For instance, if you are debating the existence of ghosts, people think that you only need to define the word "ghost."

This is false – it is even more important to define the word "existence."

If you are trying to debate whether doughnuts are food, defining doughnuts is less important than defining what food is.

There is a larger category called "existence," and a subcategory called "ghosts" – there is no point defining "ghosts" unless you first define "existence." You cannot compare a null with a null, or a null with an object. If I define a doughnut exactly, and then ask you whether a doughnut is in the category "Flibber," surely you will tell me that the question cannot be answered.

For all comparison debates, all terms need to be defined to the satisfaction of all parties. (Once this is achieved, the debate is usually concluded very easily.)

Requiring definitions is our most fundamental weapon against sophistry. Sophists avoid definitions and utilize colourful language – "Mankind shall not be crucified on a cross of gold!" – in order to sway the emotions of the audience, and so bypass their reasoning abilities.

Any time you see someone rush into a debate without first defining terms – or refusing to be pulled back to the starting gate in order to define terms – you are, most times, viewing a ghastly, manipulative sophist.

I learned this first while debating in high school and college, but later learned it much more painfully during my 15 years as a software programmer and entrepreneur.

Specifications are the design elements of a potential software program. If specifications are agreed upon by programmer and customer, then the software can be built for a tenth of the cost. In other words, changing specifications *after* the coding process is underway costs 10 times as much. And software is much less important than **The Argument**.

Consider a common debate in society: "capitalism promotes inequality." Most people jump in at the deep end – truly a hole with no bottom, save the end of civilization – and start arguing about the current system, and how to promote "equality," and so on.

Capitalism simply means property rights, and free trade without coercive interference. This definition is so incredibly far removed from the current Western economic system that calling it "capitalism" is like describing a random stabbing as "emergency surgery."

For instance, Western governments enforce a coercive monopoly on the creation and distribution of currency, which is the lifeblood of all savings and investment and trade. If there is no free market in money, there is no free market all.

Also, what on earth do people mean by the word "inequality?" Do they mean inequality of opportunity, or inequality of outcome? Inequality of height? Or beauty? Or intelligence? Or ambition? Or perseverance? Or dedication?

In a running race, if everyone starts at the same place, that is equality of *opportunity.* If you want everyone to *finish* at the same time, that is equality of outcome. And in order to achieve that, you must change where people start, or assign various burdens to the fastest runners.

(Here's a hint: "social justice" means equality of outcome; "justice" means equality of opportunity.)

Also, in any field of human productivity, a tiny minority of people produce the vast majority of output. This is described as a Pareto distribution. In any productive group, the square root of the workers produces half the product. This means that if you have 10,000 employees, 100 of them produce half the value. This basic fact undercuts any argument for egalitarianism of outcome.

Also, when people argue "capitalism leads to monopolies," what exactly are they talking about?

What is a "monopoly"? Is it a voluntary preference that most people choose in the free market, or is it achieved through government force? Is it a monopoly like voluntary monogamy within a marriage, or is it a monopoly like being locked in a crazy person's basement?

In debates in general, very few participants seem to have a clue – not only about definitions – but also about the essential requirement to even *have* definitions.

When people talk about government, what are they talking about? Do they define "government" as a voluntary organization that reflects the reasoned will of the people, or is it the central coercive monopoly within society?

Without definitions, all is prejudice and manipulation.

For instance, if the word "capitalism" remains undefined, then what fills in the definition for you?

Why, your *emotions* of course!

If you like capitalism, you will think of it as free and voluntary trade. If you don't like capitalism, images of exploitation and domination arise within you like Dickensian ghosts.

If you are religious, the word "God" summons within you beatific images of universal power and benevolence. If you are an atheist, you see only a big mental squiggle of epistemological contradiction.

If the word "equality" conjures images of the hungry being fed, the sick receiving medicine, the poor being housed, and so on, then you respond positively. If, on the other hand, the word brings to you images of totalitarian control, economically suicidal central planning, and mountains of dead bodies, well, you get the idea…

Debates without definitions tend to magnify the existing prejudices of those in the audience. Those looking for cheap applause and the syrupy suicide of irrational confirmation bias avoid definitions like the plague. Those seeking truth and reality – in general, that which *opposes* the self-serving biases of the masses – demand definitions.

Naturally, this does not mean that they will actually *receive* definitions, but putting in the requirement is an essential first step to eventual credibility.

Complexity and Definitions

The more complicated the debate, the more necessary the definitions. There is a meta-definition necessary for all debates – hardly ever acknowledged – which is: what on earth is the *point* of a debate?

Almost a decade ago, I produced an 18-part *Introduction to Philosophy* series, wherein I defined the terms most necessary to philosophy – truth, reality, error, argument, fact, evidence – from the ground up.

The purpose of a debate is to compare **The Argument** to the truth. Either person may succeed, both persons may fail, but they cannot both succeed, since having a debate means taking opposing – or at least incompatible – positions. In any clash between two incompatible positions, only one can potentially emerge victorious. If we are lost, and you say "go south," and I say "go north," we can't both be right.

The *terms* of the debate are far less important than the *purpose* of the debate. The *purpose* of the debate is to compare **The Argument** to the truth: the methodology requires definition, reason and evidence.

The question of whether or not God exists is the juxtaposition of the concept of God to the empiricism of the senses, since we must understand that ideas in the mind are not the same as things in the world. God certainly exists as an idea within the mind; God certainly exists as a belief system; churches and Bibles and priestly smocks all exist; and religion has particular consequences to those who believe in God. But none of these issues are central to the question of God's objective existence outside the mind.

Concepts do not exist outside the mind, *contra* Plato. The abstract mathematical purities of a perfect circle, or $22 \div 7$, or an infinitesimally small point, or $E=MC^2$, do not exist in the tangible material realm, any more then you can drive across the idea of a bridge, or live in the concept of a house. In other words, a dictionary is not a mall.

The Argument is a conceptual explanation of things in the world. Where **The Argument** does not touch the world, it remains futile, abstract, merely *self-referential* (for me, the greatest condemnation of a theory!).

The debater does not fundamentally test his propositions against his opponent, but against *reality*. If you are arguing with a friend about the best way to get to Las Vegas, you are testing your propositions against empirical geographic reality, not against each other. If you win **The Argument** with your friend, but end up heading in exactly the wrong direction, have you really won **The Argument**? The immediate battle may be against your opponent, but the ultimate war is against unreality, anti-rationality, anti-empiricism. You can easily win the fight, but lose the war.

The purpose of **The Argument** is to get to Las Vegas, not to get your way. We wish to emerge victorious against error, not a mere opponent.

If your goal is to get to Las Vegas, losing **The Argument** if you are wrong *gets you to Las Vegas*.

If your goal is to win **The Argument** – for reasons of vanity and insecurity, no doubt – then you would rather lose your way than lose **The Argument**!

Madness.

There is no way to win **The Argument** about the best way to get to Las Vegas without referencing the external world, without maps, GPS, or even looking out the window. The debate is the comparison of the propositions to reality, to truth, to objective, empirical facts.

To take an example we are all familiar with: imagine you come to a 'T' in the road and you turn on your GPS, but you don't know whether to go left or right. Your GPS generally cannot help you, since it cannot determine your direction prior to movement. You say go left, your friend says go right, and the GPS will shortly tell you which way is correct.

You see how important this is? You have a proposition, a hypothesis, an argument – go left, or go right – and objective reality determines which argument was – and is – correct.

It is possible that either going left or going right is the best course of action, since neither option is logically contradictory. However, if you say, "go left *and* right at the same time," this would be a silly and unhelpful joke, since it is logically self-contradictory. If you say, "go down," you may be inviting a romantic response, but you will certainly not be getting any closer to Las Vegas.

The logical consistency of your proposition is necessary, but not sufficient, for truth. Truth, since it reflects empirical reality, cannot be self-contradictory, because empirical reality is not self-contradictory.

You cannot go left and right at the same time: this is internally self-contradictory. Digging straight down will never get you to Las Vegas, so this is not internally self-contradictory, but instead contradicts empirical reality, which is that Las Vegas is on the surface of the earth.

If Las Vegas is 100 miles to the west, and you go east (and are willing to buy an airplane ticket), you could conceivably loop the planet and arrive back in Las Vegas. When we say, "Which way to Las Vegas?" we are really saying, "Which is the most *efficient* way to Las Vegas?" It is not helpful if someone answers our question by adding thousands of unnecessary miles to our journey.

BUILDING THE CASE

Almost all human conflicts result from a lack of clarity in definitions. Foggy definitions do not come about by accident and are rarely advanced honestly. A refusal to rigorously define terms generally arises from a preference for dominance, control and sophistry, rather than any honest belief that such definitions are a waste of time. If you have time to waste in pointless arguments, surely you have time to spend defining your terms.

For society, just as for an individual, definitions are destiny. If you define yourself as a failure, you will never succeed, at least in the long run. If you define a task as impossible, you will never achieve it.

If foggy definitions can be promulgated in emotionally positive terms, the non-argument is generally won. For instance, if I can define "justice" as "using the government to take money by force from the rich and give it to the poor," then socialist-style redistribution becomes inevitable, because who wants to stand against justice, *amirite*?

If I can define "healthcare" as "government-run healthcare," then socialized medicine becomes inevitable, because who would want to deny healthcare to those in need?

It works the same with "charity," or "helping the poor" – if these can be defined as government welfare, the non-argument is won in favor of the state. If "education" can be emotionally redefined as *government* education, all is lost (or won, if you are the state).

Of course, it is impossible to legitimately, rationally and rigorously define all these activities as only existing within the sphere of government power. Charity is voluntary, taxes and government redistribution are not. In order to absorb all these activities into the realm of government power, two arguments need to be made – though they are rarely made explicitly:

1. Those who correctly identify the coercive reality of state power must be mocked, downplayed and ignored.
2. It must be endlessly implied that these beneficial actions cannot exist in the absence of state power.

The first argument must be made because everyone instinctively understands that a voluntary action can be virtuous, but a compelled action cannot be. The introduction of compulsion into voluntary human affairs is immoral, just as the introduction of compulsion into sexual affairs is the moral difference between rape and lovemaking, and just as the introduction of compulsion into dating is the difference between romance and kidnapping.

The second argument exists as a backup line of defense against those who overcome the first argument, and who understand the coercive essence of state programs and actions. The first argument claims that it is moral for the state to compel people to be good *by hiding the compulsion*. The second argument is pragmatic, or consequentialist, in that it claims that this compulsion is necessary, because without it, people would suffer. The sick would not get healthcare, the poor would not get charity, the hungry would not get food, the ignorant would not be educated, and so on.

If you disagree with the first argument, you hate virtue. If you disagree with the second, well, you hate the needy and want them to suffer.

Since the forced redistribution of wealth involves trillions upon trillions of dollars, representing unimaginable heights – or depths – of political, social, educational and media power, it is quite clear *why* rigorous definitions are studiously avoided by those standing with leathery language whips over the befuddled human herds across the world.

It is also clear why those proposing rigorous definitions can sometimes get into more than a little bit of trouble.

The need for definitions has been clear for thousands of years – certainly since the days of the pre-Socratics in ancient Greece – and yet clear definitions are almost never advanced or negotiated during an argument. Nine times out of ten, clear definitions resolve **The Argument**: if you can clearly define God, and clearly define existence, resolving **The Argument** becomes as simple as putting a key into a lock and turning.

If you can define compulsion, and define virtue as voluntary, then all initiations of compulsion are the opposite of virtue. They are immoral or evil.

See how easy **The Argument** becomes when you have clear definitions?

See how important it is for sophists to *avoid* clear definitions?

THE ARGUMENT AND EMOTIONS

Building an argument is so easy that it is hard to understand why it is so rarely done. Thus we must talk about our emotional resistance to clarity, cohesiveness and comprehension in language.

Philosophy is like a worldwide GPS: everyone enters a destination, and then turns and goes in the exact opposite direction. For years, I found this confusing and thought I just needed to improve the maps and the directions, so to speak. Now, after a half-century on this planet, I understand why people fear and oppose clear definitions as the basis of *The Argument*.

Over the past 150,000 years that we have existed as a more or less distinct species, our emotions have been finely tuned by our need to survive *within the tribe*.

Our capacity to reason is generally pointed at *reality*, not the tribe. Our objective reasoning abilities allowed us to master fire, build primitive structures, develop weaponry, and eventually create civilization itself, albeit sporadically at times.

Human beings are highly susceptible to manipulation; the natural world is, in general, not. (Nitpicker's might cite the domestication of animals as an exception, I'm happy to grant that, with the caveat that it took thousands of years of selective breeding for neoteny to triumph.) You cannot talk a chicken into giving you more eggs, but you can convince a chicken *farmer* to give you eggs, if in return you offer him paradise in the afterlife, or a spell for good crops, or a love potion, or a reprieve from being murdered, or other such incentives.

A rock does not want to survive, and therefore cannot be talked into moving out of the way. Human beings *do* want to survive, and as social animals, we need the support of the tribe in order to survive and reproduce. Therefore, we are susceptible to social pressure.

Cats are largely solitary animals, and so cannot easily ostracize each other; wolves are tribal, and so are far more susceptible to social pressures. Cats can hunt alone; wolves need the tribe to bring down prey. Young rabbits rocket to maturity within weeks; human babies need 20 to 25 years for their brains to fully mature. We possess giant brains as a trade-off for our unprecedented levels of helplessness as infants and toddlers. We can think partly because we lack claws and big teeth and armoured hides. Our primary predatory strength is our brain, which has cost us speed and strength and bodily weaponry.

Thus, because we are susceptible to ostracism, and can neither survive nor reproduce effectively without the cooperation of the tribe, social approval is literally a life-and-death matter for us.

Conformity to existing tribal rituals and belief systems is therefore necessary for survival, but conformity also comes at a significant cost.

Belief systems that harden into immobility over time prevent progress within a tribe or society: think of the multi-thousand year stagnation of Chinese civilization, which vastly outstripped European civilization for millennia, and then fell behind and became susceptible to European influences and manipulations like Marxism and US foreign policy in the 1940s.

Tribal belief systems fall into the category of the Aristotelian mean: too much rigidity breeds stagnation, but too little rigidity breeds chaos and decay – such as Western countries are experiencing right now.

Tribes with few stable or foundational belief systems have little in-group preference, little reason to sacrifice for the collective, little pride in the defense of their mindset or culture, and thus tend to be overrun by tribes with more stable and foundational belief systems.

In the West, at least, respect for tradition is important, but challenging tradition is also important, providing Western civilization its fairly unique blend of conservatism and experimentation. Free speech is one such example. It is a foundational idea that facilitates the challenging of existing values. Science is another example: it possesses a fundamental methodology that regularly overturns existing beliefs about the nature of matter and energy. We can also include the free market in this category; the creative destruction of innovation and free trade is a conservative methodology that produces radical changes in society.

Challenging and overturning existing tribal beliefs is a reproductively risky strategy, to say the least. If you are a man and you challenge the foundational beliefs of a woman, she might reject you. Do this enough times and *all* women reject you: whatever genetic predisposition to challenge beliefs you possess dies with your bloodline.

In other words, if you are a bachelor, challenging tribal belief systems is identical to exposing yourself to a predator prior to reproduction. Too much original philosophy serves the function of turning you into a eunuch. (Occam's razor, indeed!)

Originality, Ostracism and Tribal Dependence
Throughout history, hunters preferred squirrels and chipmunks and mice to prey that could fight back, but you can't squeeze a lot of calories out of

a mouse, so sometimes it's worth hunting bigger prey, despite the danger. You bring down a moose in winter, you eat for weeks; a chipmunk is barely a snack.

In the same way, if you redefine tribal definitions, or adjust its arguments, significant resources can flow your way. You may overturn and replace an existing priestly or aristocratic class, or even a warrior class. (Think of the relationship between the Communists and the Romanovs in 1917.) You become an epistemological rock star, with many groupies to choose from. Challenging and redefining tribal norms is the most rewarding – but also the most dangerous – hunt there is. Think of Jesus challenging the temple priests.

(In general, men challenge social norms more than women, for a variety of reasons I've talked about at length in my podcast. You can find more details in Charles Murray's book *Human Achievement*.)

For many of you – particularly if this book engages you – the prospect of hunting social norms is very exciting. I guarantee that when you enter the arena, you will feel some trepidation as well. This is healthy, natural, and good. It is good both to hunt and for the hunt to be opposed.

The vast majority of people will not only never challenge social norms, but will actively resist any challenging of those social norms. This is also healthy, natural and good. Evolutionarily speaking, mutations only work if the vast majority of the organism does *not* mutate. If everything mutates at the same time, you get some god-awful biological mess that cannot draw breath.

(But enough about modern art...)

So, if you are interested in **The Argument**, you will be excited to hunt, yet cautious of backlash.

Although it has become cliché to talk about ideas in biological terms, it is still worthwhile to remember that current belief systems exist as ideas, as well as genetic and epigenetic manifestations: they are giant super-organisms that fight like any other organisms to protect their existence and capacity to reproduce. Genes for irresponsibility invent socialized medicine in order to avoid the inevitable free market consequences of bad lifestyle decisions (70% of health ailments result from lifestyle choices). Taxpayers do not expect to subsidize the gambler's debts, but the sexually transmitted diseases and illegitimate children produced by casual sex are paid for by society at large.

Less intelligent people invented democracy (more intelligent people invented Republics), because, being less intelligent, they could not influence society through the brilliance of their writing and oratory. But naturally they wish to have such influence, and therefore invented the concept of "one adult, one vote." This makes their political perspectives equally valuable to the greatest genius in the land. In other words, they get the *effects* of genius, without the genetics or hard work of *becoming* a genius.

From an amoral, biological standpoint, who can blame them? If you can gain influence without effort, you gain reproductive value for your biology and mindset at virtually no cost: at least, in the short run. If you have a problem with this, you have a problem with evolution, which brought us here in the first place.

In the long run, democracy produces the welfare state, which produces more unintelligent people, which requires lowering educational standards, which dumbs down the population as a whole, which dictates the intellectual levels of art, movies, books, television – and culture, which produces the endless vanity-pumping idiot-praise of artistic endeavors. The intelligent do not like to be praised – particularly by the unintelligent – but the unintelligent love praise, particularly by those they consider intelligent.

The welfare state gives the unintelligent a vastly disproportionate share of the national income, which creates a giant market for stupidity. Many "artists" are more than willing to lower their standards to serve this emerging market. The intelligent invent technology, which makes it much cheaper to indoctrinate the masses. Streaming services are available for a few dollars a month, and the less intelligent are endlessly praised and pandered to, further diminishing any desire they might have to improve their capacity to think.

Stoner movies, hedonism praise, cool losers, you get the idea.

As the less intelligent vote to consume more and more social resources, the more intelligent have fewer resources they can use to actually sustain – let alone improve – society.

If you remember the Pareto distribution – a small subset of workers produces half the output – you can see why wealth tends to aggregate disproportionately in society. Society should praise its most efficient farmers and thank them for all of the wonderful food they produce, but the less intelligent among us fall prey to sophists who tell them that it is unjust and unfair that some farmers get rich, while other farmers stay poor. The "solution" is to take money from the productive and give it to the unproductive, which creates a slow death spiral of destructive incentives and disincentives.

This is what happens when we reject **The Argument**.

We all have to make decisions about our resources, time, ambitions, energies, focus, the scant and finite days and hours we have in this world. Either those decisions are made voluntarily, or they are imposed on us through force. I will either earn the money I need, or steal it: either directly through theft, or indirectly through the mechanism of state power.

I began this book by saying that **The Argument** is life itself. You may have thought this hyperbole, but I assure you it is not.

Freedom is freedom from force. We resolve our differences either through **The Argument**, or through force.

Freedom is **The Argument**, and **The Argument** is freedom. Freedom creates and sustains billions of human lives the world over.

When we reject **The Argument**, we reject freedom.

When we reject freedom, we reject the conditions necessary to sustain billions of human lives.

End **The Argument** and you end billions of lives: consider Soviet Russia, communist China, and modern-day socialist Venezuela.

When the poor steal from the intelligent, the intelligent stop working to make life better – and often even possible – for the poor.

When the poor use the state to steal more and more resources from the intelligent, those resources are generally squandered, which means fewer resources in the future.

Freedom means letting smart people do smart things. Rejecting freedom, rejecting **The Argument**, means that society quite quickly runs out of resources.

And then, the poor do not do very well at all.

Populations swell because of freedom, because of **The Argument**. When freedom and **The Argument** are rejected, the resources that support the increased population begin to vanish.

This results in a shrill, universe-wide invitation for the four horsemen of the apocalypse to take up residence in the land.

Billions of people thrive because of freedom: when freedom is rejected, population falls through war, famine, plague, and criminality. Nature adjusts, spurned virtue has its revenge, and bodies start piling up, seemingly endlessly.

Expecting the less intelligent to understand and anticipate all of this is a fool's quest. It is to act less intelligently than the less intelligent.

Asking someone with an IQ of 85 to understand the long-term dysgenic and deadly effects of his next welfare check is truly asking the impossible.

It is not kindness to bring people into the world in order to starve them, sicken them, or destroy them through war.

This is the power of understanding **The Argument**: **The Argument** is *life*, it is civilization, it is sustainability, it is peace, it is wealth and plenty – it is survival itself.

If we look back through history, we see that dedication to **The Argument** fosters the growth of civilization, while the abandonment of **The Argument** destroys civilization.

The Argument enables life; compulsion destroys it.

WHY THE ARGUMENT IS OPPOSED

Since **The Argument** reflects empirical reality, and empirical reality is rational and consistent, **The Argument** must be rational and consistent with empirical reality.

Universality

The first test of any theory that claims to reflect reality is *universality*. A theory of physics cannot apply merely to Melbourne Australia, or the dark side of the moon, from 2 to 4 AM Eastern Standard Time.

Thus "is it universal?" is the first question you must ask of your argument

If it is not universal, it is not an argument; it is merely a statement of subjective preference. "I like ice cream," is not an argument. "Ice cream contains dairy," *is* an argument, since it claims to describe a property objectively measurable and testable within empirical reality (not merely subjective perspective or preference).

"Inequality is bad," is not an argument, but a statement of mere personal preference: "I do not like inequality." People often substitute a moral word or phrase for something they emotionally dislike. Instead of saying, "I do not like inequality," they say, "inequality is unjust." Inevitably, when you ask them to define the word "unjust," it ends up being a synonym for their negative emotional experience. In other words, saying that you don't like something is not a universal statement, and certainly not a moral statement, which means that people will not generally rush to solve the problem that makes you feel bad. If, however, you can convince people that what makes you feel bad is in fact some form of evil, then many will join you in your fight against this supposed "evil" – which is really just your negative emotional experience. Moral claims are, most times, a call for others to solve your emotional problems. (Think of the word, "problematic," which generally means that you are emotionally troubled by some situation. But rather than being honest about your emotional troubles, you pretend that you are morally disturbed by some "immoral" situation. (More on this below.)

In the realm of morality in particular, universality is key. As described above, arguing that everyone has a right to a job cannot be universalized, since some people must be providing the jobs, and some people must be filling them. The same can be said for the right to a "living wage." Creating opposing categories for the same conceptual group is not only irrational, it is directly and corrosively *antirational*. Defining animals with mammary glands as both mammals and the opposite of mammals is the mark of a biologist who needs to be institutionalized.

Thus, before embarking on an argument, you must ask yourself: *can my argument be universalized?*

To take a modern cliché of the left: non-whites cannot be racist. Can this be universalized? Really, think about it, before you read on...

Everyone can be racist. Adding the silly "racism is racism plus power" does not rescue the theory, since racism is a state of mind, rather than a manifestation of political power. Also, the black boss of the white employee has power, as do the black political leaders in South Africa, many American cities, many African countries, and so on. It is a boringly silly argument, a horse that breaks its leg trying to get out of the gate.

In the same way, the communist argument that capitalists exploit workers is also boring, because in a free-market both parties are voluntarily selling their labor and resources to each other, with no direct compulsion on either side. In a free-market, wages are part of **The Argument**, since both parties can walk away from the negotiation without threatening violence.

Men exploit women, according to some, because housewives don't get paid for their labor, which is complete nonsense, of course: housewives most certainly *do* get paid for their labor, in that *their husbands pay the bills for the house they both live in.* If you doubt this, go mop and tidy an abandoned house in the woods, and wait for groceries to magically pile up in the broken fridge.

THE ARGUMENT AND BEING UPSET

The king – I should probably say 'queen' – of modern make-believe counter arguments is the "I'm upset!" dodge.

This can range from the innocuous ("that's inappropriate!") to the catastrophic ("hate speech laws!").

Being upset is not an argument; offending politically correct sensibilities is not an argument, neither is conforming to them. Being upset only provides information about your emotions, not about the quality of **The Argument**.

Women experience stronger emotional responses to negative stimuli - for instance, being contradicted in an argument - than men do. One research study (Sex differences in effective fronto-limbic connectivity during negative emotion processing) found that:

> "Subjective ratings of negative emotional images were higher in women than in men. Across sexes, significant activations were observed in the dorso-medial prefrontal cortex (dmPFC) and the right amygdala. Granger connectivity from right amygdala was significantly greater than that from dmPFC during the 'high negative' condition, an effect driven by men. Magnitude of this effect correlated negatively with highly negative image ratings and feminine traits and positively with testosterone levels."

As University of Montreal Department of Psychiatry Associate Professor Dr. Stéphane Potvin explained:

"A stronger connection between these areas in men suggests they have a more analytical than emotional approach when dealing with negative emotions. ... It is possible that women tend to focus more on the feelings generated by these stimuli, when men remain somewhat 'passive' toward negative emotions, trying to analyze the stimuli and their impact."

Thus, high-reactivity people are often not responding to your argument, but are responding to the *negative emotions that your argument provokes.* They are not trying to find the truth; they are trying to manage their own hysteria.

When the emotional centers of the brain light up, the rational centers of the brain go dark. This, of course, does not mean that women can't argue, or that men are always rational, but it is important to understand the physiology of emotional reactivity, otherwise you will very often end up thinking you are having an argument, when you are not.

Women in general also experience social disapproval as more harmful than men do, which is why they tend to avoid giving offense, and view being offended as some sort of rebuttal.

As the influence of women in society has grown, so has pragmatism, which can also be called *consequentialism,* which is the idea that an argument can be judged by its effects. If the effects are negative, **The Argument** is "problematic" or "inappropriate" or "offensive."

None of these are rational terms – what does it mean for an argument to be "problematic"? It means nothing, except that it is uncomfortable, or might trigger negative emotions in someone. The word "inappropriate" also indicates some form of mismatch – "this is the inappropriate tool for the job." What does this mean?

"Trigger warnings" often require others to change their behaviors to manage an audience's emotional reactions.

Basically, all this means is that avoiding negative emotional experiences is more important than achieving the truth. Any truth worth pursuing provokes discomfort, because all the easy truths were discovered long ago. If discomfort justifies rejecting truth, all we are left with is anodyne clichés.

Intellectually, conforming to reason and evidence isn't that hard – the great barrier to **The Argument** is not intellectual, but *emotional*.

This can be frustrating, if you have actually achieved self-mastery, but it is an aspect of human nature that we should have some sympathy for (but which we should not indulge).

Throughout our evolution as a species, the act of opposing tribal superstitions generally got you killed – or at least ostracized – which often has the same result for your genetics.

Furthermore, tribal rulers – from chieftains to kings – often sent out spies to root out potential treason. They would sidle up to you and try to get you to confess to being in possession of rational and objective thoughts. Then they would betray you and end you.

For many reasons, being on the receiving end of a rational argument provokes great anxiety in the majority of people. This is not because of a lack of integrity, but rather the desire for life and reproduction built into all living things. We are all here because our ancestors were cautious. This caution and anxiety in the face of ideas that challenge tribal superstitions should not be dismissed as immoral, but respected as an essential survival mechanism.

Of course, superstitious beliefs don't recognize themselves as superstition, but rather appear as "rational" to those who hold them. If that "rationality" opposes base sense empiricism, then a "higher reality" is invented, where irrationality has magical consistency and all contradictions merely represent an alternate form of integrity. This means that superstition always portrays itself as rationality, which provokes inevitable hypocrisy when empiricism undoes the illusion.

This was required for our survival, in times of war and famine, plague and pestilence. We can always claim intellectual superiority by pointing out the hypocrisies of necessary evolution, but the basic reality is that we are only here to claim such superiority because of prior adaptive hypocrisy.

Understanding this does not mean we forgive all deviations from reason and evidence, but rather that we understand their unfortunate prior necessity.

In other words, **The Argument** is usually very easy to resolve, once definitions have been agreed upon, and Stone Age emotional baggage has been cast aside.

Ah, but that is the trick now, isn't it?

Why The Argument Is So Hard: Tribalism and Reason

We are not designed for truth, or objectivity, or rationality, or empiricism – we are only and forever designed for *survival*.

To a large degree, survival does involve processing truth, objectivity, rationality and empiricism – and we have developed faculties to utilize these strengths in the pursuit of survival, but that is not *all* we require.

Biologically speaking, that which is more complex takes longer to develop. The most complex entity in all of nature is the human brain, which takes a ridiculously long time to develop. The male brain reaches maturity a quarter-century after birth, the female brain a few years before that. The lengthy helplessness of human babies is unique in nature: we can do virtually nothing for ourselves for the first year or two of life, which can be considered our "fourth trimester." Our brains grow as large as they possibly can within our mother's wombs, and then we exit that joyful abode shortly before the size of our heads would split our mothers in two.

This near-bottomless dependency and helplessness requires enormous amounts of social cohesion to give us the best chance of survival. Babies and toddlers must constantly be monitored and breast-fed, which means other members of the group must hunt for food and feed and protect mothers.

Also, mothers with a stronger bond will more likely ensure the survival of their offspring, and voluntary mating produces a stronger bond. A victim of rape will have a lower emotional investment in her offspring. Thus, at least in more advanced and sophisticated societies, rape is not how families are formed.

Therefore, since impregnation is voluntary, women are free to choose potential mates according to markers for mutual reproductive success. Since she requires significant tribal resources in order for her children to flourish, she will be more likely to choose a man who obeys tribal norms.

In order to gain access to the essential resources of tribal support and cooperation, tribal norms must be obeyed. Even something as simple as being guarded while you sleep requires the cooperation of others. And if others have a value to offer you, they can make legitimate demands upon your allegiance, or obedience. If your neighbor picks up your mail while you are away, he has the right to ask you to do the same. This does not mean you must do so, but if not, you'll most likely have to make other arrangements the next time you go away.

Children who did not conform to tribal norms generally did not last very long, or breed very successfully after they reached sexual maturity.

Two factions generally enforced tribal norms – male elders, and youthful females. Young women were heavily indoctrinated into tribal norms, and told that breeding with men who did not comply with those norms would result in ostracism, which was essentially gene death.

Young males were inculcated into tribal values by elder males. Young women were inculcated by their mothers, and the combination produced highly stable (some would say *static*) tribal norms.

Our conceptual ability developed according to the requirements to conform to tribal norms as well. If a witch doctor offers an imminent benefit for subjugation to social rules, the benefit is testable. If you are offered a sunny day tomorrow in return for obedience today, and it rains tomorrow, then your desire for obedience will be blunted. The further in the future your promised benefits arise, the less testable they are.

However, the further off your promised rewards are, the greater they need to be (the basis for interest rates, of course.)

This leads societies to eventually promise a paradise after death, which is not empirically testable in the here and now. This leads people to think of immortality and morality and gods and all sorts of other highly conceptual entities.

Our conceptual ability may very well have grown out of escalating bribes for obedience to tribal norms.

The Argument and Conformity

We are designed to conform to the demands of both objective reality and tribal customs, although these two factors rarely conform to each other.

If we reject empirical reality, we do not survive: we cannot hunt effectively, protect ourselves from predators, build shelter, farm, or gather nuts and berries, etc.

If we reject tribal norms, we do not survive, either directly, in that we die without the tribe's help, or indirectly, in that we cannot mate, or our off-spring are ostracized.

Thus, attempting to unite empirical reality and tribal customs can be seen – and I believe is emotionally *experienced* – as a dangerous form of predation.

We strenuously avoid trying to bring rationality to tribal customs, because in the past, this generally resulted in personal or genetic death.

The anxiety and stress we feel when facing a dangerous predator – a giant shark, a grizzly bear, a hungry pride of lions – mirrors the anxiety and stress we feel when philosophy attempts to bring reason to tribal customs.

This basic reality is how we can understand the extraordinarily strong emotional reactions that erupt from people whose irrational beliefs are challenged by reason and evidence. Throughout most of our evolution, reason and evidence could get you killed. Most people waited until they were old to tell the truth, and often spoke bitter truths out of despair and hatred. Some, like Socrates, revealed so much of the anti-rationality of his society that his last words before drinking his death-penalty hemlock were:

"Crito, we ought to offer a cock to Asclepius. See to it, and don't forget."

Asclepius was the God of medicine and healing, and suggesting a sacrifice indicates that Socrates felt gratitude for being healed – but of what? Not necessarily of life itself, since according to Plato, Socrates never spoke of life as a disease. Most likely, he was grateful to be "healed" of the ignorance of his peers, who voted to put him to death.

A dedication to reason and evidence has significant negative evolutionary impacts.

You might think that this hostility to reason and evidence is true for religious communities, but that scientists and atheists welcome the rigors of reason and evidence: but you would be wrong.

The Argument and Atheism

Atheists claim to respect reason and evidence, but substantially inhabit the "large government, high taxation" clusters of the political spectrum – mostly on the left, of course.

Atheists generally condemn theists for believing in something that does not exist – a deity – while at the same time atheists generally believe in something that does not exist – the state. Atheists believe that theists become less moral by subjecting themselves to writing in a book, but atheists want more and more government laws to force obedience in society. Atheists point at a parliament building and think it is proof that the government exists, but laugh at a theist pointing at a church to prove the existence of God.

Atheists claim that you do not need a God to be good, but recoil at the idea of people being good without endless coercive state laws.

This is because atheists have formed a typical ostracism-based community, with enforcement by elders – the so-called four horsemen of atheism – and with sexual rejection for nonconformity by young females – the social justice warriors who will not date you if you support Donald Trump, for instance.

Theists often conceive a punishment for noncompliance with religious edicts called "hell." Socialist atheists create a punishment for noncompliance with political edicts called "prison," which may be considered somewhat more immediate and vivid than potential negative experiences in the afterlife.

Atheists deride the theist concept of social ostracism for noncompliance, and then ostracize and attack those who question atheistic devotion to the state.

Christianity peacefully accepts the rejection of Christianity – there are no laws punishing ex-Christians, or non-Christians – but atheists do not accept the rejection of state compulsion: you disobey the state and you go to jail. Statist atheism – *statheism* - is an infinitely more dangerous superstition than Christianity.

Naturally, particularly if you are an atheist, you will say that atheism is not a belief system, but rather the rejection of an irrational belief system. While this is certainly true in a narrow technical sense – atheism is to ideology as baldness is to hair color – the unfortunate reality is that, statistically, you are many times more likely to be on the left if you are an atheist than if you are a Christian. If atheism is a neutral rejection of an irrational belief system, then atheism should not be statistically associated with any other irrational belief system. But this is not the case at all!

You may also say, as is usually the case with people who dislike a particular argument, that correlation does not imply causation, but you would be wrong about this too.

If atheism were a mere coincidental belief, only accidentally conjoined with statism, then atheists would have no problem admitting the irrationality of their state worship. In other words, if no correlation existed between atheism and statism, then atheists would not be hostile or anxious when faced with the irrationality and outright danger of worshiping the state. Emotional resistance proves causality, because it shows a deeply ingrained and passionate preference for a particular viewpoint. Human beings worship about 10,000 different gods: if I become very upset about the disproof of only *one* of those gods, we know which god I was raised with, which god I still believe in.

Human beings generally believe that society needs strong leaders to dominate wayward personalities, and keep them in strict line with social norms. This inevitably results from irrational belief systems – we do not need religious enforcers to remind people of gravity, or to take umbrellas when it rains, because basic reality needs no reinforcement.

However, when social beliefs fly in the face of rationality, empiricism and objective reality, then people must be kept in line through violence and ostracism. (I know, I know – I argued for ostracism earlier, but not *forever*. Ostracism is essential only when facing the accumulated historical antirationality of our local culture. When irrationality is replaced by philosophy, exasperated ostracism will become largely unnecessary. When was the last time you needed to ostracize someone who was pro-slavery?)

Christians choose ostracism – usually as a last resort – atheists choose the violence of the state.

Ostracism is a voluntary barrier that ensures that only the most dedicated social activists get to alter the trajectory of the local culture. You have to really believe in your principles to court and overcome ostracism. State censorship is too high a barrier, and virtually ensures social and intellectual stagnation.

What irrational beliefs do atheists possess that require an addiction to the coercive powers of state enforcement?

While a tantalizing topic, we shall leave that for another time.

OVERCOMING OBJECTIONS TO THE ARGUMENT

When faced with emotional hyper-reactivity to **The Argument**, what are we to do?

I don't have any objective or provable answer to this question, but I will share with you my experiences gathered over more than three decades of public and private debates.

When we are faced with anxiety from another person, many of us have a tendency to want to comfort that person, to minimize their emotional discomfort.

Quite often, this is *entirely* the wrong approach.

If you were on the phone with a friend walking in the jungle, who suddenly faced a jaguar on a tree, would you tell him not to worry at all? That everything was going to be all right?

Of course not, unless you wanted to listen to that person getting killed.

If someone was gathering resources to climb Mount Everest, would you tell him not to worry, that everything would be fine, there was no need to be so alarmed or cautious?

Again, unless he was a mortal enemy, you would sit down with him and go over every conceivable disaster scenario, in order to help him prepare as much as humanly possible to survive the adventure.

We may gain short-term emotional relief from talking people out of their anxieties, but that often comes at the expense of long-term disaster.

Since the beginning of my public conversations about philosophy many years ago, I have made the following speech on a more or less regular basis:

> *Philosophy is dangerous. Philosophy can even be deadly. Dedicating yourself to the pursuit of truth through reason and evidence puts you on a direct collision course with many, many people around you, with your tribe, with your society, and all of its imagined values. Staggering amounts of social resources – economic, religious, political – are tied up in the promulgation of highly profitable stagnant fantasies. Challenging these fantasies not only provokes wild emotional reactions, but threatens the existing allocation of trillions of dollars, through the welfare state, through subsidies, the military industrial complex, tax breaks, regulations, you name it. Animals generally fight viciously – even to the death at times – in order to protect their resources. Many people in society will react to your challenging of their false beliefs as strenuously as a farmer watching in horror as you set fire to his crops – because in many ways the analogy is a direct one. While it is true that the pursuit of reason and evidence may lead to deep and abiding happiness – reason leads to virtue leads to happiness – there is no guarantee of this, although there is a certain guarantee of significant emotional trials and threats and ugliness and rejection, should you take this path. I prefer that you take this path, as should countless others, since the more of us there are speaking reason and evidence to irrational power, the*

more quickly we can be victorious in the spreading of truth – but I do not want you to be unprepared for the difficulties that lie ahead. I would rather you not take the thorny and fiery path of philosophy at all, than take it and then abandon it, which leaves you floating in a dangerous social and emotional void, and only serves to empower those opposed to philosophy, since they will be able to claim another victory, another person turned from the truth, which strengthens their future opposition to all who set upon this path, and weakens the will of the strong to step upon it. So embark if you want – and I certainly want you to – but be fully aware of the dangers that lie ahead, of the steely strength you will need to stay on the path, of the staunch companions you will desperately need at times, of the hostility and rage the truth will provoke, which will be aimed at you, because nobody wants to be seen as openly hating the truth. Join us, we beg you, but know what battles you are approaching: forewarned is forearmed.

Now, you might think that this dire injunction would warn everyone away from the pursuit of philosophy – but again, you would be wrong.

There are hardy souls among us who love little more than a challenging fight, a well-defined enemy, and the deep satisfaction of slamming evil. There are warriors among us who would scarce rouse themselves from bed, were it not to grip a sword in their eager palm. There are those among us who prefer a life of virtuous combat to sleazy ease. There are those among us whose hearts recoil and rebel at submission to petty ir-rationality, and who would no more bow to antirational social conventions than they would kneel before the scant majesty of a dead mouse.

These powerful hearts and minds are not frightened off by talk of chal-lenge and difficulty and danger, but rather smile broadly, strap on their armor, sharpen their swords, and march with deep song into a battle they do not yet know they were born to win.

And the very sound of that deep song, and the glint of their weaponry, causes most foes to scatter before them. The victory is in the courage, not the fight, because courage so often wins the fight simply by showing up.

So – *show up*. That is all history has required, and all the future demands.

PART TWO: HOW TO DEBATE

Now, we are ready.

In order to *have* **The Argument**, we must first understand what **The Argument** *is*, because if we do that, most arguments can be resolved before they even start.

We embark upon **The Argument** in order to compare two propositions – not to each other, but to the truth, to reason and evidence.

The Argument is often perceived as one person versus another, a form of gladiatorial combat. This is worse than misleading. **The Argument** is beholden to a third party – the *truth*. Think of two merchants attempting to sell their wares to a king. The king chooses one, or both, or neither. The decision of the King is what is relevant: it can be affected by the presentation of the merchants, but they do not decide the sale, they merely offer up their goods.

This is how we avoid making our own positions overly personal. When I engage in **The Argument**, I am not attempting to dominate the other person with my personal position. If it is a personal debate, I am attempting to bring reality to him. But I am more than willing to have reality brought to me, should it turn out to be on his side.

In a public debate, the goal is not to bring reality to your opponent, but rather to the audience. If you are play fighting with a friend while practicing to be a boxer, you do not fight with all your might to dominate and destroy your opponent. On the other hand, in the ring, for a championship bout, all pretence of friendship must be dropped: you are in it to win it.

When publicly debating, you are not attempting to disprove your opponent's position, but rather to overthrow the illusions of the audience. Think again of a boxing match: your goal is not to beat your opponent, but to win the necessary points from the judges, since that is how you win. Your real opponent is not the other boxer, but the negative judgement of the judges.

Due to this, I am much kinder in personal debates then I am in public debates, just as I would be more gentle when play fighting with friends than if I were boxing in a championship ring.

Since **The Argument** is designed to bring truth to potential friends – in a personal debate, this is your debate partner; in a public debate, it is the audience – we must examine the methodology of the debate, to understand how best to achieve our goals.

If we forget that the truth is the judge of the debate – the third-party we must satisfy in order to win – then we view **The Argument** as a battle of personal wills, and lose sight of the goal.

The Argument rests on the following essential premises, or axioms:

1. Arguments have the potential to be objectively better or worse.
2. A better argument is one that more accurately reflects objective reality.
3. Objective reality is both rational and empirical.

4. Therefore, a better argument is one that is more rational and/or supported by more empirical data.

Due to the above realities, there can be no argument regarding the following:

1. Objective truth exists.
2. Objective truth requires conformity to reason and evidence.
3. Objective truth is universally preferable to falsehood and/or incomprehension.
4. Language can effectively and accurately interpret and describe objective truth.

If **The Argument** is attempted with no requirement to conform to reason and/or evidence, then you get soul-destroying conflagrations of verbal abuse, escalations, manipulations, caustic jokes, and all other sorts of base or sophisticated linguistic treachery.

It is utterly pointless to play at a game with no objective standard of victory or loss. Would you enjoy chess if it just involved randomly shifting pieces around the board, with no standard of winning or losing? It would not even be a game. The triumph of objective truth through reason and evidence *is the standard of winning and losing in* **The Argument**. There is no point watching a debate if there is no capacity for either party to win or lose, or for any and all methodologies to be accepted as valid, including revelation, hunches, word salads, insults, speaking in tongues, or who is the better juggler.

Since **The Argument** is usually verbal in nature – and always language-based – language must be capable of describing and establishing a pathway to objective truth. If language has no capacity to encapsulate or define objective truth, then **The Argument** becomes impossible. It is like trying to play tennis with words, as comically described by Tom Stoppard in *Rosencrantz and Guildenstern Are Dead.*

If language is largely meaningless, then trying to win an argument is like trying to drive a nail into a wall with the force of your insults. Wrong tool, wrong job, wrong position.

There can be no debate about the existence of objective truth, or the necessity of reason and evidence in its pursuit, or the value of truth, or the potential objectivity of language.

If you bring a bazooka to a tennis court, you might be playing some form of horrible game, but it is definitely *not* tennis. If you bring nihilistic scepticism about truth, reason, evidence, the value of truth, or the comprehensibility of language to **The Argument**, you may be playing some form of horrible game, but it is certainly not **The Argument**.

I would no more participate in a private debate with a nihilist than I would participate in a tennis match with a man wielding a bazooka.

Truth exists. It is attained through reason and evidence; it is infinitely preferable to error; and it is accessible through language.

This is the root of **The Argument**, plain and simple.

Deny any of these, and you are no longer part of **The Argument** – you are, in fact, in the way of **The Argument** and an enemy of civilization.

Truth Exists?

The relationship between metaphysics and epistemology can be slightly tricky, although relatively easy to navigate if one retains basic common sense. So, let's take a short build-from-the-basement detour to establish the fundamentals.

Concepts have no existence in the objective, empirical world – truth is a relationship between *concept* and *evidence*.

As a child, you looked at drawings of the solar system, with grossly enlarged planets travelling on thin white rings around the yellow sun. The orbit of the planets was represented by circular lines around the sun: but no one – at least I hope – told you that the planets ride orbital lines like a monorail.

Planets go around the sun, and we describe this as an orbit. The planets exist, the sun exists, gravity exists as an effect of matter, but "orbits" do not exist. They are a mental description of the paths taken by planets around the sun, balanced between inertia and gravity.

If you have three coconuts, you have three distinct entities in the real world, but you do not have three distinct entities wrapped up in the shadow of the conceptual number "three." The coconuts exist, but the number "three" exists only as a conceptual description within your mind, not as an empirical entity.

This relationship between concept and object seems very complicated to us as adults, but is easily solved by infants as early as 6 to 8 months after birth. Babies cannot grasp quadratic equations, but they can easily understand the relationship between concept and object. Try telling a child that you will give them a PS4 for Christmas, have them open a box to find "PS4" written on a piece of paper, and their tears will demonstrate that they know the difference between idea and object.

We get confused, or more accurately, we are confused by sophists wishing to exploit us, by the relationship between *concept* and *object*. We imagine that just because something exists only in the mind, it must necessarily be subjective. However, if we sturdily tie concepts in the mind to objects in the world, then concepts become objective, at least to the degree that they accurately reflect objects in the world.

Imagine the object is a statue, and the concept is its shadow. Clearly, the shadow is not the statue – but equally clearly, the shadow is neither random nor subjective. The shape of the statue, combined with the angle of the light and the contours of the earth, objectively produce the shadow.

Alternatively, imagine making a drawing of a statue: clearly the drawing is not the statue; it is usually smaller, and two-dimensional rather than three-dimensional (though both exist contiguously through time). But this does not mean that we can never judge the accuracy of the drawing. If I try to make a drawing of a man on a horse, but it looks exactly like a cat on a rainbow, I have not made a very good drawing, at least not of the man on the horse. The drawing is not the man on the horse, but its accuracy is not purely subjective.

Language and the Truth

Turning to language, we can become even more precise. Every drawing I make of a statue of a man on a horse is inaccurate to some degree: even a photograph misrepresents to some degree. However, if, when I come home, you ask me what I have been doing, and I tell you that I have been making a drawing of a man on a horse, this is perfectly accurate. I have made a drawing, attempting to reproduce the statue of a man on a horse: nothing about this is imperfect.

If you have not seen the statue, you might have a slightly different idea of exactly what I was drawing, but whatever idea you had, it would still be of a man on a horse.

You see how this works? We check the accuracy of our concepts by comparing them to what they describe. Since concepts are derived from entities in objective reality, they gain the category "objective" by accurately describing objective entities or attributes.

A shadow is not subjective, although it is not the statue. A drawing is not subjective, although it is not the statue. And a concept is not subjective, although it is not the entity. Modern art does not make this claim for objectivity or accurate representation of the external world. In general, these artists paint impressions or feelings or specifically anti-empirical non-representations. In this way, the accuracy of the art can never be ascertained, except by the pretentious. This unfortunate development resulted from the invention of photography, and the resulting drop in commissions for artists, which prompted artists to seek state subsidies, and thus disconnect themselves from the market, i.e. from service to their culture.

The Art of Erasing The Argument
If you have half a shred of common sense, what I discussed above makes complete sense. (I know that is not an argument, but I get to make that statement because I have already made the arguments above).

I think it's fair to say that babies and toddlers have half a shred of common sense, and they understand all this easily and completely.

This of course begs the question: why is this basic common sense not obvious to everyone? The answer will surprise you, because I'm sure you already know it.

Counterfeit Arguments
I want you to think of yourself as a currency counterfeiter – not in the legal sense, like a central banker –but in the openly illegal sense. Obviously, the

more accurate your currency appears, the more likely it is to be accepted. If you scrawl a bunch of numbers on a piece of toilet paper, you're not going to get very far as a counterfeiter.

As a counterfeiter, you are a parasite on legitimate currency and your enemy is *any person or process that can detect your counterfeit currency*. You require that value be created outside of your counterfeiting, in order for your counterfeiting to have value.

You counterfeit because you can detect what has real value – money – but your counterfeit only has value because other people cannot detect what has no value, i.e. your fake bills. The perception of value is required, but must also be denied. (This self-contradictory perspective is one reason why we know it is immoral. For more on this argument, please see my book *Universally Preferable Behaviour: A Rational Proof of Secular Ethics*, available at www.freedomainradio.com/free.)

Creating counterfeit bills takes labor, but less labor than actually earning real money, otherwise there would be no point doing it. Counterfeit bills only have value because other people *don't* make them. The more counterfeiters, the less value each counterfeit bill has, both because they raise the value (and risk) of detection, and because an excess of currency triggers an increase in prices. The word "inflation" actually means an increase in the money supply; the resulting increase in prices is merely the effect of that increase.

If only a single counterfeit five-dollar bill was in circulation, there would be no point training employees on how to find counterfeit money, or investing in machines designed to expose it, because the cost of training and investment would be far higher than the potential losses of getting a single false five dollar bill.

The number of counterfeiters in society generally reaches equilibrium. They multiply until countermeasures make the value of additional counterfeiting diminish to the point of pointlessness (the law of diminishing criminal returns).

The natural enemy of the counterfeiter is the accurate detection of counterfeit money – any machine or methodology that accurately reveals fake money diminishes the value of counterfeiting.

Counterfeiting – particularly in modern times – is a complex and detailed process, requiring significant investments of time and money. An accurate counterfeit detection machine renders all that investment fairly valueless.

Imagine you walk up to a store with a counterfeit $20 bill (and you know it's counterfeit, because you created it that morning, in your basement). You are quite sure that the bill will be accepted – until, standing in line with your purchases, you notice that there is a strange new machine right beside the cash register, and a sign that says: *100% guaranteed counterfeit bill detection.*

Immediately, you feel uneasy – your palms sweat, the hairs on the back of your neck prickle. Could it be real? 100%? Surely not – it must be some sort of trick, a fake machine that pretends to ferret out counterfeiters, *Inception*-style.

Suddenly, you are in the position you hoped to impose on the cashier. The cashier hopes that every bill she collects is valid, but is afraid some are not. You now hope that the counterfeit detection machine will fail, but fear it will work.

You have three choices. You can abandon your purchases and flee the store, hoping to find another store without such a device. But, if more and more stores get these devices, and they work, your predation is largely at an end. (Also, what if the store does not advertise that it has such machine, but uses it anyway? Oh, horror!)

You can attempt to use your bill, and hope that the counterfeit detection machine doesn't work. If it does, you can pretend to be outraged and claim that it is a false positive, and perhaps even brazen it out with the police, if they are called, and insist that you had no knowledge the bill was a counterfeit. However, that can quickly become a sticky situation. Also, if you claim to be in the accidental possession of a counterfeit bill, it will be more risky trying to use another one in the same neighborhood, because it would show a pattern of behavior that would be increasingly hard to ascribe to mere bad luck.

Your third choice is to attempt to get information about the accuracy of the machine without directly putting yourself on the potential path to prison. You could go up to the cashier and say that you think the bill you have might be counterfeit, and ask her to check it. If the machine fails, you have some evidence that it is not 100% accurate. If it succeeds, you can ask her to please turn the bill over to the police, and try to make a smooth exit. However, this does have some risk, since most stores these days have security cameras, and you may be identified by the cashier to the police. Also, the police will likely question you about where you got the counterfeit bill, leading you down a thorny path of instant lies, possibly to your doom.

Sophistry Versus Philosophy

I am, of course, talking about the relationship between the sophist and the philosopher, between the manipulator and the thinker, between those who pursue control, and those who pursue truth.

The sophist is a seducer, not a lover. The seducer just wants to get into your pants and will say anything to achieve his goal, other than admitting that he will say anything to achieve his goal. The sophist has a hidden goal of self-profit, which he clouds in a murky fog of pretended virtue. The politician who thirsts for power over your money tells you that he aims for the general good. Sophistry is the pursuit of a dishonest goal by dishonest means: the methodology is not objective, not rational, not empirical, but rather seductive, manipulative, and vicious, especially if you seek to expose the mendacious machinery of linguistic theft.

The philosopher starts with a blank slate, and builds the case carefully, consistently, and rationally. He welcomes disproof, just as you welcome a GPS telling you that you have overshot your destination.

The sophist starts with an end goal – which cannot be honestly stated – and works backwards to figure out what needs to be said to gain your bamboozled acceptance of his pretended position.

A painter studies painting and nature. A counterfeit painter studies the painter he wishes to counterfeit. The painter studies in order to create beauty, while the counterfeit painter studies in order to steal from the genuine painter.

The philosopher studies arguments; the sophist studies the effects of arguments. The philosopher studies reason; the sophist studies people. The philosopher aims at truth; the sophist aims at control.

When rationally contradicted, the philosopher expresses gratitude; the sophist manifests rage.

If you disagree with a philosopher, he moves on in peace. If you oppose a sophist, he summons allies to destroy you.

You may flee a philosopher because you fear the truth, but you flee or appease a sophist because you fear the sophist. A philosopher is motivated by love of the truth, knowing that the truth is required for love. A sophist is motivated by a cowardly greed for unearned resources.

The enemy of currency is not poverty, but counterfeiting. The enemy of philosophy is not ignorance, but sophistry.

The Origins of Sophistry

Sophistry has two fundamental origins: one innocent, one guilty. Since we are currently in a civilizational phase of innocent sophistry, we will start with that.

In the movie "Castaway," Tom Hanks opens a coconut with the blade of an ice skate he found washed up on the shore of his deserted island. We don't think that he is a fool for doing this, but rather applaud his ingenuity in making the best use of the tools he has available.

In the absence of the best tools, we make the best of the tools we have.

If parents believe that children are fundamentally irrational, and need to be controlled through yelling or hitting – and that failing to control them in this way actually harms their children – then as surely as a period follows a sentence, parents will end up yelling at and hitting their children.

If people believe that without coercive government redistribution of wealth, the poor will die in the streets, then they will generally vote for the welfare state. A man rarely uses a barrel as a boat, unless it is the only flotation device available.

We all have to make decisions in society – both individually, and collectively. We need our children to learn self-restraint and conformity to sensible rules; we need to negotiate chores, vacations, finances and parenting in our marriages; we need to decide how to use the coercive power of the state to best organize society in the long run, or whether to use it at all.

We all have to make decisions, everyday, all the time. Even if we are stripped of **The Argument**, stripped of reason and evidence, told that everything is subjective and there's no such thing as truth, these lies do not stop our endless need to make decisions: all they do is force us to make those decisions *without reason or evidence*.

We can drive with our eyes open or closed, but we cannot stop driving.

We are going to be making journeys – as a species, we can never stop making journeys – our only question is whether we make our journeys blindly, or with maps and satellites and GPS feedback.

In the absence of **The Argument**, we resort to tricks and intimidation and seduction and force and manipulation, all the hell-sent baggage we must sort through to get things done in a world does not respect **The Argument**.

Parents need their children to stop hitting, start sharing and eat their vegetables. In my own experience, this is best achieved through peaceful negotiation, generous parenting, patient explanation, consistent integrity, and continuous examples of parents eating vegetables themselves. The behavior of children mirrors their environment. No one teaches children every word they know, for the most part they pick up language through immersion and exposure. If you want children to do something, do it consistently yourself. If you want children to not do something, consistently don't do it yourself.

However, the endless lie that children are irrational and emotional and prone to wanton acts of self-destruction – that they throw tantrums without cause and are monsters of couch-surfing, sugar-seeking, screen-staring immature appetites who need forcible restraint and aggressive parental control – gives rise to a brutal form of totalitarian parenting, which in turn gives rise to the perception that voters are like children, and governments like parents. If people are not forced to be good, they will be bad.

Also, many of the rules inflicted on children by parents, teachers, and society as a whole are frankly irrational. In the absence of philosophy, rather than admit the irrationality of many social rules, adults instead escalate aggression in order to compel conformity.

To understand this, imagine the following scenario: you receive a phone call informing you that some horrible personal disaster will be inflicted upon you unless you run into the street and get the first person you meet to say "flibertyjibit" (and you cannot inform this person of the threat).

Let's say you have good reason to believe the threat real and grab the first person you meet, demanding he speak these nonsense syllables.

This person – let's call him Bob – will be alarmed, frightened, and recoil from your manic insistence, but you cannot let him escape until he repeats the garbled phrase.

What do you do? Will you offer bribes, threats, pleas, and what if he threatens to call over a nearby policeman? How will you get your way? How will you save yourself?

This is the state of the world today: desperate need, but no arguments.

Children are told what to do, but are rarely provided reasons – either because adults don't know the reasons, or the reasons simply don't exist. So children are bribed, neglected, punished, threatened, hit, scolded, nagged, all to ensure compliance with the garbled phrases of irrational traditions.

This is not to say that all traditions are irrational, but the way we inflict traditions on our children is usually irrational.

Children thus learn that size and power and strength must be obeyed, that might makes right, in other words. This forces them to grow up in a world where conflict is generally win/lose – like two flat pieces of paper pushed together on a table: one ends up on top, the other on the bottom. If you want to have your way in this world, you must have power and authority, you must bribe or frighten people into complying with your will. Sadists rise to the top, masochists serve their needs, and moral souls abandon the game.

Children learn very quickly that in society decisions are made with manipulation, flattery, and intimidation, and if you want to win in the world, that's what you need to do. Those willing to threaten and bribe get their way, while those who don't get plowed under, exploited, robbed, bullied and mocked. In this world, there are farmers and livestock. Resources flow to the most aggressive and manipulative, and away from the cautious and the thoughtful. Vanity and megalomania rule the world; humility and rationality make you a slave.

Bullies who cause trouble are transformed into victims, while their actual victims are labeled oppressors and exploited.

Society jeers at the reasonable, and cheers aggressive hysteria. The irrational mob charges from victim to victim, hoisting thinking heads on spikes as a clear warning to anyone who might even *think* of trying to put two cogent thoughts together.

Many raised in such a world are sophists out of desperation – by default almost – and many, given the choice, would do almost anything to escape the soul-corroding, acidic fogs of false and manipulative pseudo-arguments: in other words: **sophistry**.

This was not always the case, however. Reason *does* win the day at times, and some societies are based on it throughout history. **The Argument**, like a phoenix, rises again and again. But since **The Argument** looks like a vampire to the true vampires of sophistry, it must be killed, again and again. Many sophists today are relatively innocent, but many sophists in the past worked fiendishly to exorcise what they perceived of as the demon of reason. The irrational, the nihilists, the power junkies – those whose moral, emotional and intellectual natures have adapted so entirely to the manipulations of sophistry that there seems to be no way back to the light – all these soulless talkers infest words like termites into the wooden foundations of civilization. What seems immeasurably strong is consistently rotted out from underneath, until the present near-collapse.

Ignorance is a form of innocence. Now that you have read this book, you are no longer ignorant. If you do not strain with all your might to fight for the return of **The Argument**, you may no longer claim innocence, my friend.

The sophist produces counterfeit arguments: they resemble real arguments – they are designed to mimic genuine arguments as closely as possible – but they are not real arguments. Counterfeit arguments are perceived to have value only because there are genuine thinkers out in the real world using real arguments to approach real truths.

Counterfeit arguments use pretend values to destroy real values, just as counterfeit currency uses pretend money to destroy real money.

Philosophy is the counterfeit detection machine, which is why it is so endlessly opposed and attacked in society, which is still substantially built on the shaky foundations of sophistry. Sophists both desperately need and desperately damn philosophy. They need philosophy to legitimize their counterfeit arguments, but they hate philosophy's power to expose them as sophists.

The number of counterfeit arguments seems nearly infinite, and swatting them feels like attempting to rid the world of flies with only one flyswatter, but a few of the most major ones are worth examining.

Intimidation

Anyone who has been on the receiving end of baseless slurs such as *racist, sexist, misogynistic, homophobic, Islamophobic*, and so on, has surely felt the sting of this brand of venomous sophistry.

Calling someone a "racist" is rather pointless to anyone with half a brain. If someone *is* a racist, pointing out the reasons why is sufficient to communicate the conclusion. If **The Argument** begins with the conclusion, it is neither an argument, nor proof of any kind.

A lawyer does not get far in a courtroom by jumping up and down and screaming the word "guilty" at a defendant, any more than a defense counsel gets ahead by screaming "innocent" over and over.

The ultimate verdict of guilt or innocence may be the result of months or years of carefully assembling and presenting of evidence, witnesses, arguments and case law. You make a case for innocence, but it is up to the jury to decide.

Starting with condemnation – or praise, for that matter – is not an argument, but an attempt to inflict a conclusion in the absence of evidence.

If you call someone a racist without clear evidence of racism, you have lost **The Argument**, because you have made no argument. If you wish to establish that someone is a racist, you first need to define what the word means – since the word "racist" means many things to many people. Then you need to establish that your definition is the most accurate of all possible definitions. After that, you must bring evidence that the person in question is acting in a manner that conforms to your definition. Finally, you need to establish *motive*, which is to say, that the person in question agrees with your definition of racism, and knowingly acts in a way that conforms to that definition.

For instance, if you believe that "racism" is the act of ascribing negative moral qualities to an entire group based on ethnicity – "Asians are untrustworthy" – but I believe that "racism" is pointing out any biological differences between ethnicities, then I might call you a racist for pointing out basic biological facts. Is that just?

Of course not.

Morality is a form of knowledge – as knowledge grows, so does moral choice and responsibility. This is why the feebleminded, children and the ignorant are given such moral latitude. If we bring a pygmy in from the Amazon jungle and place him in a supermarket, and he takes a piece of fruit, would we immediately arrest him for stealing? Of course not: he does not know where he is, or the moral standards, or the legal consequences of his actions.

If we suddenly find out that dolphins are more intelligent than we are, creatures that have solved most of the major problems of philosophy, would we still keep them as performing pets in aquariums? Of course not, even though those who kept them in aquariums surely can be excused for their ignorance.

Similarly, a toddler who takes a piece of candy from a store should not be roundly condemned, but rather instructed in the ethics of property and theft.

If I take a mint from a bowl in a restaurant, and I later find out that I was supposed to pay a quarter for it, I am not guilty of stealing, since most mints in bowls in restaurants are free.

One can be racist, without being morally responsible for being racist. If we imagine a child growing up in some anti-Asian cult, where he was told over and over about the "evil nature" of Asians, then he will grow up with strong feelings about Asians. But we would not hold him morally responsible for being indoctrinated. We would start to hold him to higher standards if he escaped the cult, but surely not before.

In the last example, we see a person whose behavior conforms to a fairly standard definition of racism, but who is not responsible for his racism, since he has no alternate frame of reference. This is analogous to excusing a colorblind man for failing to distinguish between neutral blue and green.

It works the same way in criminal law. For a man to be convicted of murder, he must know the definition of murder, that murder is wrong – and have voluntarily murdered someone. Failure to meet any or all of the standards does not mean he gets to roam free in society, it just means the difference between moral condemnation and confinement for the safety of others.

If we attempt to leap over these three required steps to prove racism – racism as a moral condemnation, not as a mere description of behavior – then we are guilty of sophistry (and, quite probably of racism, for reasons we will get to shortly).

If we call someone a racist without first arriving at a consensus about the definition of racism, or proving that his behavior conforms to that definition, (and also proving that he is aware that he violates that definition through his behaviour), then we have committed a grave injustice, and revealed our own sophistry.

(Now to be fair, you have not revealed yourself as a sophist if you have done these things in the past, because, just like an unconscious racist, you may not have been aware of what you were doing, or of the standards you were violating. But assuming you cannot disprove this argument, we can begin to expect better of you going forward.)

The primary job of the philosopher is not to condemn, but to educate – condemnation comes only after repeated education is denied or avoided. Education allows us to differentiate the ill-informed from the openly malevolent. If I knock on your door to inform you of a body buried in your backyard, and you are shocked and appalled and immediately call the authorities, we can judge you one way. If you immediately hit me with a brick and double the number of bodies buried in your backyard, we can judge you another way.

The goal of the sophist is not to educate, but to condemn – to deny education through ostracism.

The sophist who screams "misogynist" is attempting to turn someone into a pariah, into a person perceived as base and evil, to be rejected and avoided and condemned. The sophist is not attempting to integrate, or educate, but to isolate.

The sophist does not want to educate people to make them better. He wants to avoid an argument by having his opponent ostracized.

A sophist is like a tennis player who, knowing he cannot beat an opponent in an upcoming high-stakes match, slips performing-enhancing drugs in his locker, in order to get him disqualified.

This is the inevitable projection of the sophist. He accuses you of what he is actually doing. In this instance, the dishonest tennis player accuses his opponent of *cheating*…

In many societies, there exist "kangaroo courts," or pretend judicial tribunals that punish enemies of the state by condemning innocent people as guilty.

In a social sense, this is exactly what sophists do.

Any tensions between new ideas and existing prejudices generally produce uneasiness and confusion in the hearts and minds of the masses. This creates a great demand for resolving that tension by condemning those who question prevailing orthodoxies: "This man makes us uneasy by asking uncomfortable questions. Please give us the mental weapons and justifications to dismiss him from our minds!" If your body is developing cancer, you desperately want your immune system to kill the cancer cells. Existing orthodoxies work the same way – those who profit from existing illusions don't want the illusions questioned, since their profit relies on others believing they are true.

A counterfeiter of currency does not attack the *concept* of currency, since he relies on that concept to give his counterfeit currency value. His attack is more on individual bills – every counterfeit dollar he introduces into the monetary system diminishes the value of all other legitimate dollars. Since he has not added to the real value of goods or services in society, his fake currency lowers the value of all real currency, triggering a rise in prices. Thus, while social wealth goes down as a whole, his individual wealth goes up disproportionately. He is willing to undermine the value of individual dollars, while requiring the value of currency as a whole.

In the same way, the sophist wins by attacking individual philosophers, while pretending to praise the concept of philosophy as a whole. By pretending to advance rational and objective arguments, the sophist relies on the perceived value of reason and evidence – of philosophy – in order to support his counterfeit arguments. By attacking an individual philosopher, the sophist gains "victory" and resources in the moment, while undermining the value of philosophy as a whole. If counterfeit currency becomes over-prevalent, the value of working for a living diminishes. If sophists and sophistry multiply – metastasize, really – then the value of pursuing truth diminishes. By attacking an individual philosopher, the sophist gains immediate relief from disproof, but only at the cost of driving philosophers out of the sphere of social influence. An excess of counterfeit currency eventually overwhelms even the counterfeiter – think of the billion unit notes of Zimbabwe, or the Weimer Republic in Germany in the 1920s, or France during the eighteenth century revolution – and eventually the counterfeiter starves alongside his accumulated victims, as can be seen in the gruesome tragedy of present-day Venezuela.

Attacking philosophers is a form of verbal human sacrifice to the ancient profitable false gods of tradition – and often, superstition.

The philosopher must be sacrificed in the minds of the masses, because his arguments cannot be disproven by the high priests of history.

In the distant past, philosophers might simply be executed; however, we have progressed as a species at least enough that we have evolved to ostracism, rather than murder.

The sins of the sophist are projected onto the philosopher. Thus, the philosopher is isolated, attacked, and sealed off from influence.

Elemental sophistry requires that the sophist project the dangers of sophism into the hearts and minds of the crowd. It is the sophist who is threatened by philosophy – philosophy is in fact the salvation of the crowd. To save himself from philosophy, the sophist projects his own anxieties onto the mob, which then turns on the philosopher to save the sophist, who in turn destroys the mob over time.

By rejecting the philosopher, the masses are able to reject the anxiety the sophist provokes in them.

The Argument and Anxiety

Any decent philosopher feels anxiety in uncovering a new and uncomfortable truth, since the philosopher is part of society and has generally been indoctrinated in the same manner.

The philosopher knows that the anxiety is worth it: although it may feel like a kind of death, he knows it will not actually kill him.

The sophist manipulates this anxiety – anxiety provoked by the death of an illusion – and translates it in the minds of the masses into the threat of literal death. Thus the sophist inflames the inevitable conflicts between motion and inertia, the future and the past – between reason and oft-deadly habit.

This is the realm of political correctness right now, the war between egalitarian fantasies and inevitably uneven realities.

The person of low ability often cannot distinguish the person of high ability, particularly in the intellectual realm. In the artistic realm – especially in popular culture – you don't have to be a great songwriter to recognize a great song; or a great actor to recognize a great actor; or a great painter to recognize a great painter – because these abilities impress themselves directly on your senses. You do not need to know the wavelength of red to know that a stop sign is red.

In the realm of moneymaking, things are very different. Statistically, most workers are less intelligent than their bosses. To the typical worker, the factory or office is magically materialized in some mysterious way by nature, and the boss just sits in his office all day making phone calls and going on the occasional business trip: all very glamorous. The manager scarcely seems to be working at all. The worker produces goods that are sold in the market – the boss merely produces spreadsheets and reports that are consumed internally. It's easy to make the case to the worker that the boss is parasitical overhead; the worker is the real producer.

The factory worker lifts the boxes and runs the machines and takes the physical risks, getting dirty and banged up, while the white-shirted boss just roams around with a clipboard, talking on the phone with his un-calloused hands. (Even the word "worker" is prejudicial – although I use it myself for convenience – since it implies that the manager does not work).

The fact that "workers" generally do not understand what the boss does is a tiny gap of ignorance that can be widened by sophists into an open fester-ing wound. They say to the worker: "*You're* the one doing all the work; the boss just sits in his office twiddling his thumbs and stealing your money."

The resulting resentment can easily race horizontally across the organiza-tional chart: since the workers don't understand the value that the boss provides, he appears an unnecessary bit of overhead, taking food from their children's mouths, offering a slap to their faces, exploitation, blah blah blah.

The boss, in telling workers what to do, often provokes resentment.

This *invisibility* – the labor of workers is visible to the boss, but the labor of bosses is not visible to the workers – creates the potential for endless discord, frustration, and unnecessary conflict. It requires the falsification of history – *workers were happy until bosses and factories came along!* – and the falsification of economics – *the rich get richer by exploiting the poor!*

The simple rule of the free market is that, in general, you are paid in propor-tion to the value you provide. Jobs that provide less value – running a ma-chine, for instance – pay less, while jobs that provide more value – finding new customers or negotiating contracts – pay more. Smarter people can do the jobs of less intelligent people, but less intelligent people cannot do the jobs of smarter people. High-level jobs generally require more time commitment, education, stress, and intelligence – thus there are fewer people willing or able to compete for those jobs. In other words, reduced supply plus increased value equals higher salary. Also, white-collar jobs don't often come with union benefits, protections and privileges; managers can generally be fired at will.

Although tempting, I won't turn this section into a treatise on economics: suffice it to say that the sophist appeals to the greed and resentments of the less intelligent, while the philosopher recognizes the beneficial value of truth in the long run, for everyone except the sophist.

Those lower-level workers who fall prey to leftist indoctrination support increased state control and regulation – and sometimes the outright nationalization – of the means of production. This results in stagnant, dying economies, the outsourcing of lower-level jobs, accelerated automation – and, in the US at least, tens of millions of working-age people not in the labour force.

Tell me, how is this beneficial for "the working class"?

Look at Venezuela, look at most of Africa, look at post Second World War India or Russia or China, and tell me that those workers were having a great time.

Letting smart people run things in the free market produces health and wealth and life – resenting and attacking smart people drives them away, causing a collapse in health and wealth and life.

Societies that embraced the free market – never perfectly, but enough – received a 70-fold increase in productivity, while halving the workday and doubling lifespans.

Do the sophists care?

No, because the sophist is to the philosopher as the bad worker is to the good manager.

The bad worker in a team provokes ostracism among his peers, who resent having to cover and fix his sloppy work. Good workers don't want job protections, because good workers are protected by, well, being good workers. Good workers don't resent the bosses, in general. They often feel sympathy for the boss who can't check out at 5 o'clock, and who has to deal with irate customers and prickly creditors and confusing accountants and lawyers and so on.

However, if the bad worker can unite the team against the boss, his own sloppy work can be more easily overlooked. If the bad worker can convince the team that the boss is malevolent, then job protections can be sought, which protect the bad worker.

In the realm of ideas, the sophist is the bad worker – he must sow resentment among his peers so that his lack of contribution is more easily overlooked. He must create a pseudo-intellectual realm of insults and manipulation, which baffle the less intelligent and frustrate the smart, so that his skill set, which is based on verbal abuse rather than careful reasoning, can win.

Many people who are good at one thing would like to see that one thing become the measure of victory in a general conflict. People who are good at shooting prefer duels, people good at debating prefer arguments, people good at running prefer races, and so on.

People good at verbal abuse and manipulation prefer sophistry to philosophy, for obvious reasons.

Sadists and sociopaths prefer sophistry.

Whatever measure you prefer reveals your true skill set. (I am good at debating, so I prefer debate, but I am making the case that this is an objectively better preference. Having come this far, you are now responsible for judging my motives and arguments rationally and objectively.)

If a man enjoys rioting and screaming epithets at people, he is confessing that he perceives himself to be better at violence and verbal abuse than those around him – and in particular, his victims.

His primary opponents will not be his victims, but rather the clear and critical thinkers who are willing to expose the vitriolic emptiness of his vicious methodology.

The sophist runs among the people, claiming that "reason" is simply a tool of exploitation by the unjust masters of mankind, that "rights" are just claims upon the forced labor of others, rather than a defense against the initiation of force, that "justice" is smashing things until you get your way, and that democracy legitimizes your hidden and predatory desires. And, should democracy go the wrong way, well, see "justice" above…

Provoking resentment through cowardly and provocative language is the essential skill set of the sophist: this goes all the way back to Meletus, who brought Socrates to trial, claiming that Socrates was corrupting the young and refusing to believe in the gods of the city: both charges not-so-subtle dog whistles to the guilt of bad parents and corrupt politicians. If you are a parent, and some stranger is easily corrupting your children, then you have not really been a very good parent at all, either because you have failed to teach your children how to think critically – leaving them vulnerable to being corrupted – or because you have been an abusive and destructive parent, which can be easily identified by a clear and consistent moralist.

As far as the charge goes of "not believing in the gods of the city" – a charge Socrates specifically denied – this is merely the uneasy and vitriolic conceit of liars and propagandists lashing back at somebody exposing the counterfeit currency of their intellectual coinage. Gods of the city = sophists.

Everything they accused Socrates of doing, the sophists were in fact doing. Projection is the essence of the sophist, who seems to believe in his core that the best defense is a good offense. The smart murderer always leads the charge against the accused murderer; the anti-moralist always exploits the highest ethical standards against the true moralist. Those who wish to destroy rights must march under the banner of rights, this is inevitable and, at this point in history, relentless.

Sophistry is based upon the lie of egalitarianism, which inherits credibility from the lack of differentiation in human physiques. An expert worker can be dozens of times more productive than an average worker, but he is not dozens of times taller. Body size is far more egalitarian than mental abilities. The genius is capable of things the average mind cannot conceive, but both brains are housed in the same general container. To the average person, the fact that a same-sized skull can contain a vastly superior mind is like imagining that an elephant can fit in a shoebox.

If head size matched intelligence, the world would be far less confused by mental excellence.

With apologies to Madonna, can you judge the quality of singing that only your dog can hear?

Egalitarianism and The Argument

If we are all more or less equal, then wide disparities of outcomes – and incomes – must result from injustice or exploitation or bigotry or some other sinister machination.

The first mark of the sophist is the suppression of information about disparities in human biology – levels of intelligence and testosterone in particular. Boys who grow up playing *against* each other quickly discover that talents and reflexes are not at all evenly distributed. I played first-person shooter video games for many years, and had a friend who could beat me virtually every single time, for reasons I will probably never fully comprehend. He always seemed to know exactly where I was going, and what I was about to do. On the other hand, the first time I played baseball, I cracked the ball skyward for a home run, shocking boys who had played for years.

Girls, who generally play collaboratively, end up seeing far less skill disparity.

There tend to be more geniuses among the male population than the female. Thinking of the bell curve of intelligence, in early puberty, the female cluster tends to look more like a vertical penis, the male spread more like a flattened breast.

Adult males end up more intelligent than women overall, by a few IQ points, and at the highest levels of intelligence, men outnumber women a dozen or more to one. Adult male brains are heavier, and contain more brain tissue than adult female brains.

For these and many other reasons, women tend to develop far more egalitarian perspectives than men, which translates into specific and often disastrous social agendas and political policies. Since women tend to favor equality of outcome, they must promote inequality in the law. If a man wants all runners to finish a race at exactly the same time, he must change – i.e. make unequal – their starting positions. You can have equality of outcome, or you can have equality of opportunity – you cannot have both.

Most people on a sports team cheer the great player who scores the winning goal, since they believe that they share in the victory.

However, because the scarcity and value of high intellect must be suppressed – otherwise the egalitarian fantasies of the sophist will be destroyed – intelligent children (boys in particular) must be relentlessly scorned and attacked: so they often isolate themselves from the average, leaving delusions of equality largely intact.

The average player benefits from having a skilled player on the team. People of average intelligence benefit from having geniuses in their society, and this poses a significant problem to the sophist. Where would the janitor at Apple be without the late Steve Jobs?

If the genius is celebrated like the star athlete, then creating resentment in society becomes much more difficult. If you know that Bob is the only reason your team made the finals, it's going to be pretty hard to hate Bob. Highly intelligent people can cause problems for sophists – they undermine the illusion of egalitarianism, and directly challenge the self-contradictory falsehoods of the sophists. (This is one reason why sophists work so hard to recruit brilliant people – i.e. *tenure*.)

If you tell people that everyone is more or less the same intellectually, then wide disparities in life outcomes become incomprehensible, which is the first small wound that needs to be worked and widened by the sophist.

It is strange, because this egalitarianism generally only shows up in the intellectual realm. Anyone who has been to karaoke night knows that there are better and worse singers; everyone who attends amateur theater knows that there are better and worse actors; everyone with eyesight knows that there are better and worse looking people. No one imagines that fat and ugly people will rise to the top of the modelling profession, or that a rare and well-made car will cost the same as a cheap and common one. No, it is only in the realm of the *intellect* that rank egalitarianism attempts to erase the natural bell curve of the species.

This becomes even more strange when you remember that people don't even have to be on the team to value the star player. The star player commands a high salary because of the millions of fans who are willing to pay his costs. The man sitting in an armchair, resting a bowl of greasy popcorn on his beer belly, cheers with joy when a star player is signed to his local team. He values the expertise of the new player, which generally *costs* him time and money (time spent watching and taxes for stadiums), and he never once imagines that the star player has achieved fame by stealing the fat man's athletic ability.

(It is also interesting, by the way, that in movies and television, the smart boy is generally depicted as physically weaker and unappealing, while the smart girl is almost inevitably beautiful.)

The fat sports fan does not feel that the sports star has stolen his abs, or his money, or his time – he is happy at the disparity of ability, cheering and celebrating it.

However, put a highly intelligent man in front of a man of average or below average intelligence, and you very often see instant resentment and hostility, particularly if the man is so brilliant that he can clearly communicate moral excellence to the average man, which creates an obligation for the average to better themselves. The sophist never demands the average person better himself, but rather provokes resentment and helps the average person blame the environment, which the sophist then offers to "fix" for a steep and soul-destroying price.

Why?

The fat sports fan knows that the sports celebrity requires innate gifts and a gruelling practice schedule. The audience enjoying an opera knows that the singers are born with great voices, which they then train through years of practice.

Turner, one of the great painters of the nineteenth century, had a famously manic work schedule. Other painters would relax into coffee and chit-chat, while Turner obsessively sketched and researched and painted. Once, when he wanted to paint a storm, he lashed himself to a ship mast during a typhoon, just to get a further sense of the power of the phenomenon. Some famous artists even dissected dead bodies, to further understand how bone, muscle and skin worked together.

The causality between innate gifts and hard work is hard to untangle. One of the reasons why hard work pays off is because it sharpens innate abilities; the opera singer practices singing partly because she has an innately beautiful voice to begin with. Innate capacity raises the value of hard work, which breeds success, or at least the chance of it.

The sophist has an instinctual ability to manipulate, to provoke resentment, to flatter the average. Many average people have a great hunger for greatness. It might be possible for them to achieve some greatness if they work hard, but most people would rather have the fruits of labor without the actual labor itself. (Human laziness is truly a double-edged sword; it is why we don't have to get up to change the channel anymore, but also why we have national debts and a welfare state.)

Some pianists are so great that they can fill concert halls and sell recordings. Some are good enough to inspire others and become teachers, while others can lead family gatherings in sing-alongs. Every level of expertise has its part to play in society: the same is true with virtue. Some educate and inspire others globally, some inspire and teach locally, and others provide an elevating example in their own personal lives.

Average people can achieve great virtues in their own lives and spheres of influence – and in particular in their parenting. Average people can consume great art – think of the 16th-century proletariat cheering on Shakespeare – and thus contribute to great art, by rewarding the artist. Average people work hard and well to create the wealth that saves the poor and enhances the great. Average people are the bedrock, the foundation, the great necessary cogs in the giant engine of society. While it is true that they are often forgotten by history, they do live on as a ripple effect in the minds of those they have influenced, and in particular, in the virtues of the children that they raise. A great orator needs an enthusiastic audience – they contribute to each other. The late great singer Freddie Mercury once said that he can only sing as well as the audience wants him to.

Average people cannot define virtue, or explore and extend it, but they can certainly *follow* virtue, as long as it is clearly explained. Average people cannot research the long-term emotional, psychological and physical effects of spanking, but they can refrain from hitting their children. Average people cannot define and prove property rights, but they can refrain from stealing. Average people cannot rationally define and justify self-defense, but they can punch a mugger.

Great minds cannot survive in the absence of the average – and great minds require their ideas to become manifest in the actions of the average. If you cannot influence the average, you have done precious little good for society, and most likely you have done great harm.

Since about the 1960s (though even earlier in Europe) philosophy, and moral philosophy in particular, has become not only incomprehensible, but *anti*-comprehensible. Postmodernism, existentialism, new wave feminism, cultural Marxism, and identity politics have all moved beyond the comprehension – and the interest – of the average person, who now views intellectuals as a vaguely sinister group of dangerously opaque tossers of word-salads.

This is the natural – and, increasingly, unnatural – result of governments paying the intellectuals, rather than requiring intellectuals to engage and provide value to average people, which would be the case in the free market. When you do not face the challenging market of average people, you no longer have to serve their needs, their interests, their preferences, or their *values*. Like a restaurant that gets paid whether people dine there or not, the focus on quality or service is lost. The socialization of intellectuals is the necessary precondition for the socialization of the masses: once intellectuals are paid and defended by the state, they tend to defend the state.

If you look at modern intellectual movements closely, you see that they are all founded upon a rejection of **The Argument**: the famous Internet meme of a young pony-tailed man screaming, "*You're a f*cking white male!*" is part of this understanding. Why does someone *not* have to listen to your arguments? Because you're a white male, because you are cis-gendered, because you have privilege, because of slavery, because of colonialism, because of exploitation, because of class – you name it, intellectuals have invented a five-dollar-word "cone of silence" spell designed to work on anyone who questions their delusions.

Rejection rather than analysis – hateful ostracism rather than thought – rage rather than **The Argument**.

The sophist does not create arguments, or respond to arguments, but *destroys* arguments. He *destroys* the capacity to debate by creating categories of exclusion designed to shut down conversation and grant victory to shrill and angry idiots.

The sophist sells the fantasy of egalitarianism to the resentful average: "You could be just like great people, except for the prejudice of great people against you!"

One of the great tragedies is that by provoking resentment, the sophist robs the average of their capacity for greatness.

It might be possible for the average person to achieve some form of greatness by substituting hard work for bottomless resentment. If you want to become an opera singer and I tell you your voice is already as great as Pavarotti's, but the petty viciousness of the people who run the opera house is preventing you from stardom, you will spend more time stewing in resentment and plotting revenge than actually improving your singing.

The sophist thus creates a self-fulfilling prophecy – by stimulating resentment, he kills advancement. If you hate and resent those whose approval you require for success, success becomes virtually impossible.

Thus does the sophist expand his market – by sowing resentment, he breeds failure, which breeds more resentment.

Furthermore, by defining success as exploitation, the sophist subtly defines failure as a virtue: *if being a boss is being bad, failing to be a boss must be good!*

By defining the world as a terrible battle between vicious exploiters and helpless victims, the sophist defines *happiness* as *idiocy*, like the Internet meme of the dog in a burning house blandly stating, "This is fine!" If the world is terrible, and you are happy, you are a fool. Thus wisdom must manifest as grim depression and resentment and rage and frustration. Only a fool grins and whistles during a firefight...

Since decent people find happiness more pleasant to be around than vengeful misery, the sophist also feeds failure by sowing division and isolation.

If we drift too far in opposition to the values we have previously accepted, we get the moral equivalent – through our conscience – of a dog's shock collar, which administers jolts if pets roam too far from a central beacon. Think of a sophist as a farmer of human division – and therefore misery, and therefore dependence – but a farmer who cannot create an obvious fence, since people may drift far from their core values, but inevitably resent being directly enclosed.

The best way to keep freedom-loving people fenced in is not to build a fence, but to tell them that it is good to stay close, and bad – or dangerous – to go far. Say "it is rational to fear a dangerous landscape." Repeat that safety is in proximity; danger resides in distance. We do not need a leash to stay close to the fire on a cold day; we do not need a law to tell us to put a hat on when it is cold.

If you can get people to invest in a particular mindset, sunk costs and confirmation bias will generally keep them lashed more tightly to that mindset than Odysseus was to the mast.

If you can infect people with the idea that success is failure, and failure is virtue, then their lives become increasingly disastrous. After a certain amount of time – not too long, actually – people end up investing so much in the virtue of failure that they can no longer question the principles that have destroyed their potential. If I have avoided success for years, taking rancid pleasure in the sordid virtue of my low state, then the agony of recognizing that I have destroyed my life and my potential and my happiness for *nothing* becomes too much to bear. When confronted with the truth, I double down to defend that which has destroyed me.

The rescue squads of the sophist's domesticated self-consuming livestock are the arguments, the reasons, the evidence – the *philosophers*. Being a philosopher is like being a doctor whose patients think he is actually administering poison. In a time of plague, the entity Death desperately wants people to believe that the *cure* is the *disease*, so they cannot be cured. In a time of increasing anti-rationality, the sophist wants people to believe that philosophy is insanity or evil – or both – so that their madness cannot be cured. The farmer says to the voluntary cows: "The woods you yearn for are actually full of wolves, the only safety is here, with me – the fences are to keep the predators *out*, not to keep you *in* my friends. Now up the ramp you go…"

The Argument and Power

Having power over others requires that they have no standards of interaction other than dominance and submission. I cannot talk a mathematician into believing that two and two make five, because the mathematician has a standard of logic and consistency that trumps mere human persuasion.

Scientists may have debates, but it is not *debates* that determine the validity of a hypothesis. The validity of a hypothesis is determined first by its internal consistency, and finally by empirical evidence. If I propose a hypothesis that gases both expand and contract when heated, no one needs to test my hypothesis to find out if it is true or false, because it is internally self-contradictory. If I propose a mathematical theorem that requires that the numbers 1 and 10 be the same, mathematicians will stop at the first line since I am violating the law of identity by requiring different concepts to be identical.

Teaching people logic – and logic is the essence of **The Argument**, since empirical evidence trumps conceptual definition or rational argument – allows them to evaluate propositions independent of persuasiveness.

We can be persuaded by others, but our most dangerous sophist is always within us. We should first direct our reason not against external persuasion, but at our own susceptibility to confirmation bias, sunk cost fallacies, and so on.

Learning how to reason, how to identify fallacies, frees us from the power of sophistry – it dissolves the livestock fences of false words, and wards off wolves with a wag of the tongue.

Teaching people to reason frees them from teachers, by allowing them to teach themselves. Good teachers are always looking for new students, because they have freed old students from the need for teachers. Bad teachers want to hang on to old students by keeping them dependent.

I have no power to convince a rational man of an irrational argument. This is the great danger that reason poses to existing power structures, and the primary cause of the absence of rational instruction in government schools, or in government curricula.

Rational thinking dissolves the chains of human bondage. It frees us not only from sophistry, but it even frees the sophists from the worse devils of their own corrupted natures. Refusing to believe a liar frees you from his lies, and it also helps free the liar from the power of lying.

It is not a great chance, but it is our only one.

Promising people acceptance if they obey – and abuse if they don't – is not an argument. Rational thinkers understand that the sophist not only fails to bring an argument, but also that the sophist *knows* he is failing and destroying the capacity of people to argue, all for the purpose of enslaving their minds and stealing their resources.

If we wish to end the domination of man over man, we must free man from men through reason, which unites our minds with reality, and therefore truth, and liberates us from the chains of dismal dependence on acceptance, or fear of abuse.

CONCLUSION: A PROMISE

Let us imagine what the world would look like if people thought *rationally*. If, through our efforts, **The Argument** wins the day, wins the future.

Imagine a world where the truth-shredding viciousness of verbal abuse no longer decided the day. Imagine a world where learned and nimble minds could peacefully and positively meet in reason and reality. Imagine a world where parents reasoned with their children, rather than withdrawing, bullying, neglecting or hitting them. Imagine a world where teachers welcomed criticism, where social solutions were proposed rather than enforced, where choice rather than submission was the norm, where unrepentant broken-record fools were excluded from social discourse, rather than vaulted to the highest pinnacles of cultural enforcement.

Imagine a world where virtue was as easy as complying with the rationality of those around you, where we no longer had to speak with caution for fear of the mob, the pitchforks, the destruction of our reputations. Imagine a world in which **The Argument** quenched the torches used to set fire to our souls for the simple crime of asking a question, or bringing to the fore an unpopular, essential truth.

Imagine a world where reporters researched difficult topics and informed us of actual facts; a world where virtue did not put us on a suicidal course of confrontation with general prejudice; a world where happiness, peace, curiosity, friendliness, acceptance – all these and more were the norm.

Imagine a world where the irrational were first instructed, and then excluded if they refused to learn, where anti-rationality was deemed a greater sin than any hysterical term of abuse that could be imagined now. Imagine if a parent who failed to teach peaceful reason to her child was viewed as infinitely worse than a pregnant woman who smoked, or a man allowing his toddler to play with matches. Imagine the gentle, positive nudges of benevolent social feedback guiding your life as necessary, rather than laws, prisons, threats, abuse, and violence.

The Argument is the gateway to this world: it is all we need to make and enter this paradise.

The key to this earthly paradise is not our physical death, but the death of sophistry.

Take everything this book has to offer and bring it to life in your own world. By loving the world enough to staunchly defend **The Argument**, we can actually create a world we can love.

Socrates brought **The Argument** to the world – and was murdered for his gift. Cornered and poisoned in a tiny cell, he viewed his death as a blessing, a release from the hatred and anti-rationality of his society.

A disease views the cure as death.

It is time we stopped trying to cure the anxiety that reason provokes by attacking the rational.

The cure for the world is **The Argument**. If **The Argument** fails, everything that reasonable minds have built through blood and suffering – civilization itself – fails.

We must defend and advance **The Argument**, or lose everything.

Now you are armed.

Go *fight*.

Made in the USA
Middletown, DE
10 October 2017